Praise for L

Lead from Within is an inspiring collection of stories from a diverse group of entrepreneurs. Each chapter shares wisdom gained, offering helpful insights for anyone's entrepreneurial journey. I especially loved reading the personal narratives of how these contributors became entrepreneurs.

— Tamara Palmer, Author and Career/Life Coach

If you've ever thought about pivoting your career and venturing into entrepreneurship, you'll find a treasure chest of wisdom, guidance and practical know-how in Lead From Within. A diverse group of business-savvy leaders encourage you to take a lesson from what they have learned and step forward with courage, integrity, perseverance and resilience.

— Jenn Baljko, founder of Always On My Way and lead author of the collaborative book *Fierce Awakenings: Calling in Courage and Confidence to Walk Life's Spiral Path*

an Anthology

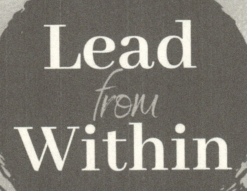

Lead *from* Within

Entrepreneurs Share
Proven Traits for Success

Lead From Within

Entrepreneurs Share Proven Traits for Success

Red Thread Books

Red Thread Publishing LLC. 2023

Write to **info@redthreadbooks.com** if you are interested in publishing with Red Thread Publishing. Learn more about publications or foreign rights acquisitions of our catalog of books: www.redthreadbooks.com or email us at info@redthreadbooks.com.

Copyright © 2023 by Kim Kleeman

All rights reserved.

No part of this book may be reproduced in any form or by any electronic or mechanical means, including information storage and retrieval systems, without written permission from the author, except for the use of brief quotations in a book review.

Paperback ISBN: 978-1-955683-97-5

Ebook ISBN: 978-1-955683-94-4

Cover Design: Red Thread Designs

The information and advice contained in this book are based upon the research and the personal and professional experiences of the authors. Some names and characteristics have been changed, some events have been compressed, and some dialogue has been recreated. Chapters reflect the authors' present recollections of experiences over time. The opinions herein are of each individual contributor. All writings are the property of individual contributors.

The publisher and authors are not responsible for any adverse effects or consequences resulting from the use of any of the suggestions, preparations, or procedures discussed in this book.

Dedication

This book is dedicated to those who taught us how to be the leaders we are today. These positive influences had direct impact and we carry that torch with great respect and appreciation.
Thank you!

Contents

Introduction	xi
1. Taking a Leap into the Unknown *When Corporate No Longer Fits*	1
Anna Cillan	13
2. Strengthening Inner Leadership *Lessons Learned the Hard Way*	15
Karen Kimsey-Sward	25
3. An Equation for Personal Empowerment *Accept Accountability — Decide — Do*	27
Catherine McNeil	37
4. Seeing Yourself as a Leader *Integrity Vision & Resilience*	39
Sierra Melcher	49
5. Six Steps to Connecting with Folks *Having Courageous and Crucial Conversations*	51
Gloria Cotton	63
6. When Leading a Family Business *How To Honor The Past, Optimize The Present, & Change For The Future*	65
Dan Gershenson	75
7. Lead From Within *Your Company, Your Industry, & Yourself*	77
Joy Poli	89
8. Four Stories *Pathways to Becoming an Opportunity Champion*	91
Lynn E. Miller	103
9. Success Traits in Action *Building a Fierce Network*	105
Kim Kleeman	115
Thank You	117
Acknowledgments	119
Red Thread Publishing	121
Other Red Thread Books	123

Introduction

By Sierra Melcher

In a world where the entrepreneurial spirit thrives and innovation propels us forward, the path to success is often charted with personal stories of resilience, vision, and unwavering determination. The pages of *Lead From Within: Entrepreneurs Share Proven Traits for Success* open a door to a dynamic realm where leaders emerge from the depths of their experiences, revealing the essential traits that have paved their way to greatness.

The journey of an entrepreneur is akin to traversing uncharted waters; it is a blend of the exhilarating and the challenging. It is a journey that encompasses trials, tribulations, and triumphant moments, where one must navigate not only the complexities of the business world but also the intricate landscape of the human spirit. It is a journey that showcases the quintessential essence of leading from within.

This book serves as a testament to the power of authenticity, self-discovery, and resilience. Within these pages, you will encounter a diverse group of entrepreneurs who have, against all odds, carved their own paths to success. They hail from various industries, backgrounds, and corners of the globe, yet they share one common thread: the profound commitment to lead from within.

Their stories are not just a collection of anecdotes; they are a living testament to the traits and qualities that have propelled them forward. As you journey through these pages, you will discover the traits that have become the cornerstones of their achievements.

Traits such as:

- Perseverance
- Independence
- Drive
- Follow through
- Communication
- Willingness to learn
- Passion
- Resilience
- Opportunity Champion
- Confidence
- Vision
- Integrity
- Organization
- Tenacity

These are not mere buzzwords but the guiding stars of their entrepreneurial voyages.

Lead From Within is an invitation to explore the realms of personal leadership, to dive deep into the minds and hearts of those who have embarked on this extraordinary journey. It is a beacon for those aspiring to blaze their own trails, a guiding light for those who seek to infuse their work and life with purpose and authenticity.

Here you will uncover not just the successes, but also the struggles, the pivots, and the breakthrough moments. We hope that these stories will resonate with you and that you may glean valuable insights from these entrepreneurs who have dared to follow their inner compasses.

As you read through the pages of this book, remember that the traits of success are not merely external strategies but intrinsic qualities that, when harnessed, can lead to profound transformation in your personal and professional life. So, embark on this journey with an open heart and an eager mind, and let the stories within these pages inspire you to lead from within, forging your own path toward greatness.

Chapter 1
Taking a Leap into the Unknown
When Corporate No Longer Fits

By Anna Cillan

Breaking free from the confines of my corporate role, I embarked on a journey to pursue my long time passion for photography that I had almost forgotten. This is my story.

The Early Years

My love for photography blossomed in my early childhood, igniting a passion that has stayed with me ever since. My father worked as a civil engineer, yet in his free time you would always find him capturing precious moments through the lens of a camera. From landscapes to portraits of the family. I can even recall my father using the tripod and setting the infamous timer which at times was too quick or too slow, depending on our ages and how well we were able to sit still for a shot. But nonetheless he always had a way of capturing us in the best light. He used 35mm film, which, for those unfamiliar, required physically taking it to a camera shop for development in order to view the images. It was always such a treat to go to the mall to pick up the photos. We have an endless supply of them filling albums - and boxes when those were filled. I am grateful for these photos so we can go back and remember the time, the place, the feeling. They are our priceless memories.

I was his second-in-command, frequently assisting him by holding his camera equipment while he skillfully captured moments that were often centered around all the family activities. From holiday portraits to action shots of my sister running track and field, you name it, our whole life literally was caught in still photographs. As I grew older, my father soon trusted me to capture photos with his camera. I remember how heavy it was and that he had to hold it for me to see through the viewfinder. He showed me how to compose images and time things accordingly to capture movement. He opened my eyes to the beauty of photography. I even recall sitting on our deck with the camera secured to the tripod to capture long exposure shots of cars as they drove by. We were painting with light on film. I had no idea what he was teaching me. When I finally received the developed shots, seeing that motion drag of the lights, I was in love.

My High School senior year, I took up the role of class historian to capture photos of our graduating class with the goal to showcase the images in a slideshow for our Senior Banquet. I had the opportunity to shoot to my heart's content with all the film and development paid for by my school. How could I not?

This was my final summer at home with my family. My father wasn't exactly thrilled about me venturing all the way from Washington state to West Lafayette, In. - home of the Purdue Boilermakers. Nonetheless, he made a special gesture by taking me to the Oregon coast for a deep-sea fishing trip. It may not be what you'd expect, but both my dad and I shared a love for fishing. To make a long story short, not even 15 minutes into the expedition, I was overcome by a severe case of seasickness. Four agonizing hours later, it finally subsided. I wasn't exactly the most popular person around because, well, I kind of scared off all the fish!

Freshman year at Purdue changed me. In February of 1994, my father was diagnosed with acute leukemia and was being rushed to Seattle for emergency care the very *same* day. I was still in Indiana and had no idea where I was going or how. Thankfully my oldest sister helped me find my way home. But it was too late for all of us. He had passed away on his flight to Seattle. In an instant, our time together was tragically cut short. My desire to pick up a camera and create took a backseat in my life. I still captured photos here and there with the camera my father gifted me and continued to be the one to capture photos of the family at holidays and really for anyone who wanted a photo taken. Photography became a refuge, a way to capture precious moments while being mindful of life's fleeting nature. It never crossed my mind to pursue it professionally; it was simply a means to capture memories to look back upon.

Throughout my career, I've had the opportunity to work with exceptional companies, starting in IT Consulting, testing software, leading teams in software testing, and eventually overseeing the management of complete financial IT projects and programs, including software implementations. Life was satisfying, the salary was very rewarding, but deep inside, a lingering feeling persisted that this wasn't my true calling. Is this what I want to do for the rest of my life?

Strengthen Your Skills

In 2015, I unexpectedly found myself laid off from my long-time job with a severance package that allowed me the time and means to travel before I pursued my next gig. I booked my first solo trip to Buenos Aires to visit a friend local to the area and, in my search for tours, I stumbled upon an Instagram Walking Tour that provided tips on how to compose some really cool shots at some pretty significant places. It was also about this time that Instagram started gaining in popularity so I dove right in. I remember focusing in on a box of produce at an outdoor market and then another shot where I pointed my camera straight up on a tree-lined walkway to capture the beautiful curly branches that rested upon the light blue sky. It was during this experience that I had a moment of realization - photography is art and, most importantly, was something I deeply missed.

To further fuel my interest, I stumbled upon a photography conference that happened to be free. I had no idea what to expect and I figured people just attended to take notes. Captivated, I attentively listened to numerous talented photographers, all conducting their own breakout sessions. In the midst of this exceptional event, I approached Scott Robert Lim, who would later become one of my mentors, with a simple request – to enroll in his class.

"What? You don't have a camera?" he exclaimed.

I confess, I was an absolute novice in the world of photography. Unlike others equipped with professional-grade DSLR cameras, the simple point-and-shoot camera left to me by my late father seemed rudimentary. Instead, I opted to carry a spacious handbag, housing only a select few personal items, alongside a trusty notepad and pen.

A few people approached me, complimenting my handbag - a sure fire ice breaker. However, they quickly realized that it lacked an actual camera. (Hi...yes that's me!) Fortunately, one of these kind-hearted individuals graciously loaned me their camera for part of the breakout sessions giving me the opportunity to practice what was being taught. I couldn't help but feel like an imposter. I surreptitiously observed other photographers, desperately trying to decipher their settings. Concepts such as ISO, Aperture, and Shutter speed eluded me. I acted like I understood, but it became apparent that keeping up the act would be difficult unless I dedicated time to learn.

Within a month, after careful research and landing a new job, I pulled the trigger and invested in my very own camera. But now what? I couldn't just make a large purchase and not use it. Like what was my goal? Is this something I'd want to pursue down the line? Uh heck no...am I crazy? At that point I was never about taking portraits of people. I loved landscapes. You didn't need to tell a tree to pose. It just stood there, looking beautiful. But I knew that if I wanted to be serious, I had to learn all kinds of photography, including taking portraits of people. Back at the photography conference, I remember Scott talking about a workshop in Paris that upcoming Summer. Great! I love to travel and Paris?...wow no brainer but now after spending a massive amount on my camera gear, I was faced with the uncertainty of shelling out even more dough for maybe a hobby?

Learning from one of the very best while surrounded by the captivating beauty of this city is what made it an obvious choice. I enrolled in the workshop and embarked on this incredible journey of knowledge and growth. Every moment spent there was nothing short of pure delight, and I learned that instructing people on how to pose only worked in my favor - you get what you envision faster. Shocker! My passion for photography only deepened and I was eager for more.

On the heels of that trip, I discovered yet another incredible opportunity to attend another photography workshop - this time in Chicago: The Headshot Intensive taught by the renowned Peter Hurley. The idea was tempting, but my wallet was still recovering. Despite this, I can hear my mother's voice echoing in my mind, emphasizing the importance of education. Her unwavering support for my educational pursuits is something I am truly grateful for. Besides, with a stable full-time job at hand, why not invest in myself now and reap the rewards later on? Looking back, 2017 was a year of strengthening my photography skills. Mastering the seamless fusion of posing and lighting, along with the intricate art of expression coaching and targeted facial illumination proved to be the winning formula for my future triumphs.

Persist Through the Crossroads

June 6, 2019 was a day I'll never forget. I had been working at my job for several years and had grown to love the company and my coworkers. But that one solemn afternoon, I was called into a meeting with my manager and was told that my position was no longer needed.

"I'm sorry, today is your last day"

It felt like I had been punched in the gut. I mean, I did just successfully finish a pretty comprehensive project but it was not a battle I could fight. Admittedly, losing my job at this stage of my life was truly demoralizing. It seemed as though all the hard work I had put in had amounted to nothing. After dedicating so much time to a place that had become a second home, the uncertainty of not knowing where to turn next was unsettling. But...

"When one door closes, another opens" - Alexander Graham Bell

After a week of grappling with self-doubt, I found myself standing at a crossroads, faced with two deeply meaningful choices. Should I opt for the path of least resistance, seeking a job that offers stability, predictable pay, benefits, and vacation time? Or should I choose the more challenging route—one that brings uncertainty about my next paycheck, devoid of benefits, and without paid vacation—but promises the ultimate reward: genuine happiness in my work?

Hesitant to fully commit, I persisted in exploring new job opportunities while dedicating a significant amount of time to explore photography as a full-time gig. I relied on the unwavering support of my loved ones and actively engaged in business networking groups to establish a semblance of routine and structure, similar to that of a traditional job.

Time didn't stop. Bills were right on schedule along with the pressure of a mortgage and just one paycheck left.

Overwhelmed?

Heck Ya!

Under the wise counsel of my budget-savvy mother, I embarked on the delicate task of scrutinizing my spending. Admittedly, I'm not particularly proud that I indulged in frequent dining out and way too many Amazon purchases. Nevertheless, this exercise empowered me to reorganize my financial resources and regain control. Based on her evaluation, I had a maximum of 8 months to dedicate to this photography venture before seeking new job opportunities. I had regular monthly calls with my mom to make sure I maintained and didn't veer off course. Knowing her genuine concern for my well-being, these conversations provided us both with peace of mind and reassurance that if I followed close to the plan, I would be alright.

Merely six months later, the omnipresent threat of Covid-19 arose. Everything was on lockdown and no one was interested in getting photos done - myself included. I was filled with fear, yet I mustered the courage to continue to build on this business venture despite my mother's skepticism. Seizing the opportunity during the lockdown, I took charge of revitalizing and enhancing my website, bolstering my back office systems, and more. I decided to tackle these systems early on to streamline my work. I reminisced about my days at CME Group, working with future and options products. The concept is to invest in the future state of a product. So, why not apply the same strategy to a service? Which is why I implemented the service to sell headshot sessions now at a special rate and redeem at a future date. This worked and, as restrictions started to ease, my business gradually gained even more momentum. Within a year and as more restrictions were lifted, I had doubled my income, and the following year, I tripled it! The solid foundation I had laid out proved to be immensely advantageous in the long run.

Everyone Has a Story to Tell

In my corporate days, there was a performance area that outshined them all - Building Relationships. I have always been naturally outgoing and genuinely curious about others. Building real connections with people brings me joy. It's no wonder I found myself specializing in Headshots and Personal Branding, where I can combine my people-oriented nature with my passion for capturing the essence of individuals. Right from our very first conversation, I genuinely get to know you by asking questions that are essentially part of my Branding questionnaire. Sometimes, we end up having lengthy phone conversations, so there's no need for me to send you the questionnaire separately. Meanwhile, behind the scenes, I visualize how I can bring your brand to life through captivating imagery. It's like my little magic trick!

I have a deep understanding of the discomfort that comes with being in front of the camera. However, I assure my clients that all they need to do is listen and follow my coaching on posing and expressions—I don't expect them to be professional models. Rest assured, I am here to create a calm and nurturing experience for you. In fact, many clients have compared it to a spa, as they feel fully supported and cared for throughout the process. And guess what? The imagery we create is phenomenal! Check out some of these shots!

Taking a Leap into the Unknown

When I reflect on the time spent with my late father, his relentless pursuit of perfection always stands out in my memory. Everytime I look through the viewfinder, his presence fills my thoughts, serving as a tribute to his unwavering commitment to doing things the right way, even when it's not the easiest. In fact, I often find myself sharing his wisdom with my clients. For instance, when I'm deciding on a certain look that uses anywhere from 1 to 4 lights for a shot, even if using just 1 light would achieve the desired effect, I'll recall my father's words: "If you're going to do it, you better do it right." These are the exact standards I strive to uphold for my clients, as nothing less than the very best will do!

My passion lies in helping clients authentically narrate their stories through compelling still images, purpose-built for their websites, marketing materials, Linkedin profiles, social media campaigns and even individuals wanting to create their very own personal brand. I create a welcoming, calm and fun environment that builds trust with my clients. This sets the stage for the magic of photography to unfold.

My core belief is that every client should feel like a star – because everyone has a story to tell! Guided by this principle, I personally promise to deliver the highest quality images that truly reflect the essence of my clients.

The Brass Tacks

Here's the deal. Somehow, I unconsciously or consciously crafted my roadmap to entrepreneurship. It all started with reigniting my long-lost passion for photography, rebuilding the foundation, and persisting through the hurdles along the way. It feels just like my nostalgic days of dodging spiky turtles and chomping flowers in Super Mario. (Yes, I was that Nintendo kid).

But here's the kicker. Your people. They are the real deal. While you may stumble upon them through family and friends, it's certainly worth seeking out networking groups tailored to entrepreneurs. They will have your back, providing unwavering support throughout the highs and lows of your journey. Always ready to push you to grow and innovate and, as a bonus, they even refer potential clients and help expand your business network. They become your perpetual source of inspiration and encouragement and perhaps one of the first people you call when you land that big gig. Go future you!

With that being said, I'd like to share this memorable moment. Two years after embarking on my entrepreneurial journey, my mom surprised me with a question, "Anna, did I get you anything to celebrate your business launch?"

"Yes, a whole lot of full time job listings…" I chuckle.

"Anna, stop joking, I am so proud of you. You are doing it" mom says with delight.

Two weeks later, I received a beautiful citrine pendant necklace in the mail. A necklace that I will treasure forever.

Thank you Mom for believing in me.

Anna Cillan
About the Author

Anna Cillan is a Chicago-based photographer specializing in headshots and portraiture, with a primary focus on personal branding. With a diverse clientele spanning across the nation and around the globe, her portfolio showcases a wide range of subjects, including corporate executives, artists, actors, musicians, models, and more. Anna's objective is to deliver high-quality visuals that leave a lasting impact on any platform, enabling individuals to genuinely present themselves in the digital and marketing world. In her free time, you can find her singing for a local church choir, taking group exercise classes, traveling or simply enjoying a stroll with her beloved canine bestie, Coco.

linktr.ee/annacillan

Chapter 2
Strengthening Inner Leadership
Lessons Learned the Hard Way

By Karen Kimsey-Sward

It was a beautiful summer day and I was sitting at my desk enjoying a cup of coffee and reflecting on the past 10 years. It was quite the ride with nine of those years being the best of my professional life to that point. I was part of building and leading a training company. We had experienced incredible growth, had a great team of people, and we had built a great culture with amazing clients. I was all about the work and very focused on my accomplishments. My whole vision of myself was wrapped up in work and my success and what I was going to do next.

During the tenth year, we were acquired by a venture capital company and I stayed on as the leader of our division. I didn't have a good feeling about this position and reluctantly took it because of course that was just what I was "supposed" to do. One of the key messages that was reinforced over and over to me growing up was "take care of other people first before taking care of yourself." My mom would exhaust herself serving others. I thought that was the way I was supposed to be. Just as I had thought, within the first couple of months, it was crystal clear this was not a good decision.

The company was hyper-focused on the financials at the expense of the employees. Coming into work every day was stressful and it was one of my first experiences of feeling as if I was a total failure. No matter what my gut was telling me, I just kept working harder and harder and feeling more like a failure every day. I was in a pretty dark place and was miserable but just kept going. Until one day, I became very ill and was in bed for a few weeks trying to recover. As I was lying there in bed, I realized the toll the past year had taken on me physically and emotionally. I knew at that moment I had to change things because I just could not live that way. A couple of months later, I made the best decision of my career-and walked away to focus on me. One of my first actions was to hire a coach to help me through the process of better understanding me and how to move forward. I had no idea where to start and what to do to change. I just knew I had to!

Through this process and self-examination, I realized that I spent most of my early career focused on achieving and continually feeling as if I had to keep proving myself. It was a never ending, exhausting cycle. I found that many times the work environments that I was in reinforced this and it became the way I thought and reacted. When everything was going well, I had a very healthy confidence-both internally and externally. When something was not going well, I might have looked confident on the outside but struggled internally.

I was so hyper-focused on accomplishments and achieving that I did not take the time to focus on myself to better understand who I was and what was important to me. I was so focused on what other people thought of me and what I achieved. That determined how I thought of myself at that time and it would change based on the situation. If you asked anyone to describe me, they would say I was strong and self-confident. They would have never guessed that many times I struggled with my inner confidence and would beat myself up over mistakes or when something would not go well. I did not see what others saw in me. Many times I allowed what other people thought of me to influence how I felt about myself. In situations where I clicked with someone, then I felt good and in situations where I struggled to connect, I did not do as well and would beat myself up. I allowed others to have "power" in my thoughts and actions which impacted my effectiveness as a leader.

Where have you given your power to people or situations that did not serve your growth?

A lot has changed since then; I have focused on my inner leadership and confidence as well as strengthening my "outer leadership" and recognizing that it is critical to work on both to be a genuine leader (and person). Early on I thought this was just something I was dealing with. As I started sharing my story with other leaders I realized many of us have similar struggles.

There were a few areas that I worked on with my coach that have been game changers for me. It was not a quick fix and it is something I always have to work on and keep in mind.

"Rewire" Your Mindset

This was one of the key actions my coach recommended in strengthening my inner confidence. Changing my mindset was (and continues to be) one of the hardest things to do. In general, I am a very positive person, but I was sabotaging myself when I encountered difficult situations and difficult people. My mind used to go immediately to fear and blaming myself (over and over again). It was a cycle that I knew I had to break. One of the key things I learned early on when researching mindset was that our brains register, focus on and recall negative events faster than positive ones. I learned the best action you can take to stop this cycle is to use a word or a phrase when your mind goes down a path you do not want. Mine is *STOP IT NOW!* Depending on the situation, my next step could be a couple of actions. If it is a situation that is stressful, I self-reflect. *Why am I reacting this way? What is really going on with me?* If I am beating myself up over a mistake, I try to figure out what went wrong and remind myself that mistakes are part of my journey and that is how I learn. We need to better understand our areas for growth but a continued focus on the negative is detrimental. Giving ourselves grace is the biggest gift we can give to ourselves. Why is it so easy to do it for others but not to ourselves? Changing how I think and resetting my mindset has been instrumental in strengthening my inner confidence and has helped me become a stronger leader. By focusing more on the positive and not staying stuck in beating myself up, I am more resilient, more creative and happier. I am also better at helping my team constructively work through setbacks.

Notice where your mindset is either drawn to gratitude or fear. Simply by noticing you will begin to subtly rewire your mindset.

Stop Trying to be Other People

Why is it that we can see other peoples' strengths while we have a hard time understanding and embracing ours? I have worked with a number of leaders over the years and this is a key area many struggle with. Many people are so focused on what they are not and then work hard to be someone else.

For me, impostor syndrome took hold when presenting to large groups. My business partner was an eloquent speaker who had a dramatic flair and people would gravitate toward him and give him so many accolades when he spoke. I so wanted to be like him so I would study the recordings from his speeches and try and emulate him. I could never get comfortable and dreaded speaking with him. During one of our speeches together I was so uncomfortable I almost passed out. I was stressed out before every speech and spent so much time in a negative headspace.

After one speech we did together, one of the executives in the audience walked up to me and said, "Wow your styles are so different. (I immediately thought: they were going to talk about how great he was). Instead then they said, "You make a great team because you both are very good and different. You balance each other." Those words were powerful; I realized that no matter how hard I tried I was not going to be my partner. I then made an effort to own my style and it has made such a difference. I realized that I have a positive energy and an authentic way when I speak which many people relate to. Whether it's speaking or leading, I realized how I show up every day, I need to own who and what I am. The more authentic I am, the more I can connect with people and can better lead others. As I embrace and celebrate my uniqueness, I can help others do the same.

How can you own more of who YOU ARE and where can you stop trying to be like others you admire?

Another key part for me in my journey was to create my personal vision and revisit it every year. Not just *what* I want to "accomplish" but *how* I want to show up every day and what is important to me. I have found that to be more rewarding than any accomplishment. This has helped me focus on myself and not try to be like others or live up to what others think I should be. Every year I revisit my personal vision, both personally and professionally. And think about how I can "live" my vision in the upcoming year. I also take a look at the past year and think through what worked and what did not work. It reminds me of the positive things and my growth as a person. Writing it down, reflecting on my strengths helped me to build my inner confidence and embrace my uniqueness.

How can you have a vision that guides you to the future you desire?

"Slow It Down"

One of my badges of honor is that I paid my way through college and was self-sufficient at age 17. I was a full-time student, part-time teller at a bank and an active member of a sorority. To do all of that well, I had to hustle every single day. It became a way of life for me and, when I graduated from college, I kept up that pace. As you can imagine, my bosses just loved it. I could out-work anyone and was a ball of fire. The more I was praised, the harder I worked. Initially, I loved the fast-paced environment and thrived on any chaos and loved the accolades. Add two kids, active in school activities, trying to be a good wife and friend AND trying to prove that I could do it all. Well we all know where that story ends. I could not keep it up. As part of my journey, I knew this was going to be an ongoing challenge for me based on who I am. I needed to build in routines to slow myself down.

1. Plan *Fun*. I went a number of years without taking a "real" vacation. If I did go on a short trip, I was always checking into the office and was always thinking about work during my time off. For years, I thought I could not take time-they might need me. I could not turn my mind off and enjoy time off and realized it was more of me needing work vs. work needing me. I started taking more vacations and made a true effort to not "call in." Not a surprise, the office was still there when I came back! As a result I found I was more refreshed and less stressed. I also stopped working weekends so I could be fully present with my family. This is still hard for me to do and I have found that, if I tell my team my intentions, they give me a hard time when I call in or email during my time off. If we as leaders don't take vacations and time for ourselves and use that as a badge of honor, it sends the wrong message to our teams. I found that taking time off helped me with my mindset and I made better decisions when rested.

2. Take Time to Self-Reflect. I spent years running to the next big thing. We would have success and I would not appreciate it because I was thinking about the next big deal. I realized this was a key factor contributing to my burn-out. This was not a natural thing for me to do and I have to work at this all of the time. Slowing down and getting to know myself and others as people is key to building inner confidence. At the end of every day I take a few minutes and think about the day and the people in my day. I reflect on the things that worked and the things that did not work. This helps me re-frame the day, celebrate successes and make sure that I reach out to those around me to celebrate their success. It also helps keep me focused on what did not go well and self-correct.

3. Show Appreciation and Gratitude. I learned this much

too late in my career and this is one of the things I wish I had learned earlier. Since I did not slow down, I did not even think about stopping to tell someone they did a good job or that I appreciated them. Early in my career, I thought appreciation was manipulative and "fluffy." I just knew that I did not need that and was just fine. Fast forward to a time when I was struggling with leaving a career that I loved (and a company that I did not love) and one of the leaders I was working with handed me a small notecard. She took the time to write down what she specifically appreciated about me and how I had made an impact. That moment in time truly changed me. I still keep the notecard in my wallet and smile when I see it. I now make it a regular practice to STOP and intentionally show appreciation to those around me. As a result, people feel appreciated and not taken for granted. It is a great way to build relationships in an authentic way.

By slowing down, I have stronger connections with my friends, my colleagues and my family. I am able to live more in the present and am able to show people how much I appreciate them. I have more relationship conversations vs. task-oriented conversations with my team. I am able to be in the moment and enjoy being in the moment which has helped me with stress. My decision-making is more intentional and proactive vs. reactive, resulting in better decisions.

Think of one example where you can implement each of these tools this month:

- Plan *Fun*
- Take Time to Self-Reflect
- Show Appreciation and Gratitude

Find Your Person

As a coach, one of the common themes I hear from leaders is that they feel isolated and many struggle with who they can trust and let in to have a real relationship with; someone to bounce an idea off of or someone to vent to or someone who is going to tell them the truth. Over the years I have heard so many stories of how they would trust someone if they were frustrated or wanted to run an idea by them and then they found out that person could not be trusted. I get it and I have been burned along the way as well. My advice every time is to not give up because finding those authentic relationships is such an invaluable part of your internal leadership. It could be a coach, a very good friend or a mentor. Too many times we can "get in our heads" and it is so important to find someone whom you can trust, who truly has your back, who will not judge you, will speak truth to you with love, whom you can be vulnerable with and you can bounce ideas off of. Too many times we just need someone to talk things through which can help us get another perspective. They have nothing to gain or lose and less of an opportunity for hidden agendas.

    I have a lifelong friend who I started walking with each morning. It started as just getting exercise before we both had a full day of work and kids and it has ended up to be one of the greatest gifts of my life. She is my coach, my mentor, my dear friend, my therapist all in one. Our conversations have helped me just get something off of my chest, get advice on a work situation, share my wins and losses. She was the person I turned to when I felt betrayed by someone at work. I knew she was going to listen and be in my corner. Just by talking it out to her, it helped me process the situation and react appropriately. When I was struggling with a job I loved and a company I did not love, she helped me get through it and was a great sounding board. This helped me better understand what I was thinking and feeling while talking it out to her and helped me to think through how I was going to handle the situation.

    Who is YOUR person? If you don't have one, begin to seek someone you can reach out to and rely on.

    I have come to accept the fact that strengthening my inner confidence is a journey and some days are just going to be better than others. It has gotten easier and I find that I bounce back much faster when I face adversity (difficult situations and people). Making the choice to focus on my mindset, slowing down and focusing on genuine relationships has helped me understand myself better and become a stronger leader. It is now my passion to help other leaders on their journey so they can live into who they are and focus on what is important to them so they have that inner peace and confidence.

May these lessons I have shared serve you personally and professionally to grow and evolve as a leader.

Karen Kimsey-Sward
About the Author

Karen is Chief Operating Officer for Dale Carnegie Chicago. She leads a talented team providing training, coaching and consulting focused on the "people-side" of the business. She is also a Certified Coach and a Faculty Coach with the University at Buffalo School of Management.

She has spent most of her career working with organizations and leaders helping them move to the "next level" of performance. Karen brings a unique perspective as a business owner who has been through all stages of a company's life from its founding through the various levels of growth.

She has a passion for helping leaders unlock their untapped potential and to figure out what is getting in the way. She helps them create a plan to attain their personal and professional goals and supports them through their journey.

karen@kimsey-sward.com

linkedin.com/in/karenkimsey-sward

Chapter 3
An Equation for Personal Empowerment
Accept Accountability — Decide — Do

"You only believe what you do, not what you say!"

— Ashley Kirkwood, Author of *Speak* Your Way to Cash

By Catherine McNeil

The plan was never to become a community activist, servant, or a not-for-profit founder. I never wanted to be an Author, Entrepreneur, Industrial-Organizational Psychologist, obtain my Lean Six Sigma Green Belt or most importantly be responsible for nurturing, supporting, and helping shape the lives of a niche parenting demographic, the three human beings that I birthed and leaders in the workplace.

Although that wasn't the plan, it has become my reality and it's one that I am extremely proud of. It's a big deal. I won't act like it's not but it's also not something easily obtained. No, I'm not referencing the training and educational hurdles. I'm discussing the *personal and professional leadership development* that only comes from lived experiences:

- the detractor in the workplace that almost pushed me into retaliation and self-sabotage with their antics.
- the not-for-profit sector challenges taught me how to navigate individuals in survival mode and contend with there being no such thing as an isolated incident.
- the people who mistreated me and made me feel like a bullied 9-year-old, or a helpless teenager.

Overcoming character-impacting instances like these forced me to eventually learn to ADD – "do the math."

You may be wondering, what on earth am I referencing? What's the backstory here?

Let's begin, with the end in mind:

A.D.D. got me through it all. I added.

What's the equation? **Accountability + Deciding = Do**

Let me walk you through each key element of "doing the math", the equation for personal empowerment.

A. Accepting Accountability

Unless you're capable of caring for yourself, you're incapable of caring for another.

Step One is Accepting Accountability

I became a parent at 20. I found out that I was pregnant during summer break after completing my first year at Penn State University. I was President of my campus student government, looking forward to completing a successful sophomore year and eventually graduating from main campus with honors as a Computer Engineer.

My dreams were comprehensive and elaborate:

No graduate schools. No marriage. And no children.

In one summer, my dream went to hell. I will never forget how disappointed my parents were. My mother, the oldest of four and a college dropout, cried for days. My father, a college graduate and the oldest of four, gave me an ultimatum. This non-custodial, unmarried father of two, one deceased son and me, very clearly offered to continue paying for my education, post-abortion. There was no way he was sending me back to Pennsylvania, pregnant. There was no way that I was getting rid of my daughter either. For me, it was about *accountability*. I was irresponsible enough to get pregnant, how, when and by whom I did. I needed to be responsible enough to finish what I started.

And boy did I finish.

I transferred from Penn State to City College to University of Illinois – Chicago to DeVry to Robert Morris. Over the course of nine years, I attended multiple schools, changing majors three times. Throughout those years, I had a second daughter, worked across multiple customer service-oriented industries at $6 - $15 per hour, moved out of my parents' home, purchased, and foreclosed on my first single family property.

By the time that I finally graduated with my Bachelor of Business Administration in Management, I had lived an entire life. That's how it felt, and I wasn't even 30 years old. At 27, I had my version of, what the black Christian church calls, a "come to Jesus moment."

I hit a wall: physically, mentally, and emotionally. I will never forget my senior year. I was working full time, completing a required internship, and managing a full course load. I had run out of financial aid and time. I bargained with my job to create a position that would fulfill my internship requirements; the school allowed me to attend classes across two campuses. I could see the finish line. Quitting was not an option. I believed self-care was something for the wealthy and established. I kept pushing. I burnt out. I was mentally and physically sick.

But I had to finish. And I did.

Accountability to my goals had gotten me so far, but simultaneously I had a higher accountability

Breakthrough: I learned that I was of no value to anyone, especially my young daughters, if I burnt out and became sick. I discovered what being overworked looked and felt like. I realized that there was only one me and, if anything were to happen to me, my children would be alone. I understood that my well-being and wellness were my priority. I accepted that I would continue to accomplish goals but not at the expense of my wellness. The more that I got to know myself, the more thoughtful my planning became.

Accountability looks like taking care of yourself so you can take care of everything else.

D. Deciding

Step Two is Deciding

Resolving that my physical, emotional, and mental wellness are my uncompromisable priority was the beginning of my journey to becoming the leader that I am. The road became more complex once I entered my master's program. I was forced to further address the yet developing, unhealed emotional and mental parts of myself. Looking in the mirror required me to accept a vastly different type of *accountability*. I had always been interested in psychology, primarily why people do what they do. Digging into my own psychology started a long road of healing and personal reconciliation.

Part of my accountability and self-work journey was tied to identifying what type of psychology made sense for me. I am naturally inquisitive; I had been asking questions about why I thought, showed up and felt how I had since my teenage years.

Because I was open to the discovery, and willing to apply as I grew, I learned so much about who I was and what I had yet to become. I learned that witnessing my great aunts'/uncles' rivalries, my parents' relationships with their siblings, and both losing their parents young, impacted my views on family. Especially my views on having, then raising my own. I learned that having been bullied and in domestic violence-rooted relationships impacted my career choices. It's for these same reasons I knew that clinical and forensic psychology were not realistic areas of study for me. I/O on the other hand, provided a happy median.

"Industrial-Organizational Psychology (also called I/O psychology) is characterized by the scientific study of human behavior in organizations and the workplace." (apa.org)

For 2 years, I researched, engaged and participated in every psychological theory, behavioral and personality assessment known to science, and man. Intentionally engaging in coursework that required me to continually get to know myself made me a greater leader, both domestically and in the workplace.

Deciding to understand my whys empowered me to operate in empathy and to own my biases and triggers. Once I was comfortable in my own skin, I became dangerous in the world.

My first job post-graduation afforded the opportunity to live my thesis aloud. I had been applying the learning theoretically and in personal relationships. I survived via student loans and random interim positions while in school. This full-time career development position in the not-for-profit sector was the initial testing of whether I had developed mentally and emotionally. Let's be honest. Our familial relationships can be optional; we choose to figure those out or not. The workplace does not provide an option and maintaining professional relationships can be a challenge.

I worked in the largest African American community on Chicago's west side. The program targeted males, formerly incarcerated, returning citizens ages 18-30, helping them develop their financial, digital and book literacy as well as their basic business acumen. We provided a stipend and as much holistic wraparound support as realistically possible. If you're familiar with the not-for-profit sector, you know that the budgets are typically constrained, teams are small, and one person will wear multiple hats. I found myself, yet again, spread thin. My job was to help shift the career trajectory of these young people when I could barely maintain my own home.

The not-for-profit sector challenged me to learn how to navigate individuals in survival mode, with a poverty mindset and a savior complex. At their core, everyone had great intentions. Unfortunately, the differences in experience, expectations and norms made it challenging to engage, let alone communicate. Operating in insufficiency is rarely the greatest hurdle; the ruling mindsets and actions are the actual root of the conflict. Had I not been on a journey to become a better me, that environment would have gotten the best of me.

The fight for funding and other peoples' lives is extremely difficult when your own basic needs aren't being met. Scenarios like this are all too common in underserved minority communities. Yet, we survive; we find ourselves creating opportunities by way of small businesses and local nonprofits.

The greatest skills developed during my 2-year tenure was networking and collaboration. My determination to be successful coupled with managing the lacking resources required me to be creative; I made friends across businesses and other not-for-profits. I developed an ability to barter programs, processes, and services. This positioned the curation of lifelong connections. Those same connections pulled me back into the for-profit sector, gave me a team of nine and my first official leadership title. These connections held me accountable, provided constructive criticism and, most importantly, continued to support me through my development journey.

D. Doing

Step Three is Doing

I'm owning who I am, how I show up and where I want to be. I am navigating my life with intention. I knew that mine and my family's well-being were the priority and that the road to provision was paved with resources by way of relationships. Navigating relationships with myself and others was the key to success. Implementing all I had learned and continuing to put it into practice brought it all together.

Understanding where I came from, how I developed and who I

wanted to be brings us full circle to today. I was selected to lead a team of three training managers in the student loan debt collection space. That responsibility was a lot more involved than simply managing schedules and their routine work day-to-day. The actual requirement called for streamlining a consistent training program across three uniquely different departments, growing the team to nine, staying compliant, identifying then onboarding a learning management system and developing the leadership skill set of an entire organization. *I did it; I did it well.*

Corporate Training and Development Manager was my first official people leader position, by title and salary. I was helping adults grow into their best selves, making a difference in business while providing for my family. I was winning. It was evident that I had been applying self-development. But that people piece was always an area of opportunity.

I had detractors from day one. I had to learn to navigate leading a team of my seniors by both age and experience. I had to design an uncharted path. It was a lot of on-the-job training for me. I did not get it right at every turn. I cried in frustration. I quit daily. I was also supported. I learned to swallow my pride. I learned how to play the game.

Life is filled with an abundance of unknowns. Navigating the unexpected, failing to give in to the discouragement and discomfort is a part of the growth process. That process is identical in the professional arena too. We're just tweaking the responses and reactions.

When someone challenges you publicly, threatens your authority and credibility, you cannot scream louder, retaliate, or shut down in the workplace. You can remove yourself, gain your composure and address it thoughtfully though. We can't avoid challenges and obstacles in the workplace; we learn that we should not be doing this in our personal lives either.

Anything unaddressed comes up again. And again. Personally and professionally, whatever we refuse to deal with will reinvent itself across multiple scenarios until it's addressed.

My temper is my Achilles' heel. I will separate myself before I lose it. I can walk away from anyone or anything with peace. My ability to detach is uncanny. This survival mechanism had gotten me far. Having to constantly move around as a kid. Attending multiple grammar and high schools. Losing a sibling. Never having the opportunity to truly develop roots anywhere. Never feeling like I belonged anywhere.

My upbringing unintentionally helped me to learn to let go. It never taught me to move on. Parenting and the workplace did. Children grow regardless of their parent's readiness. Whether we have the money, time, or capabilities, the child is going to develop and have needs. We must learn to provide, nurture, and produce for them despite our lack. We're not talking about money here. Children require us to be multiple people simultaneously: empathetic, an active listener, collaborative, courageous, accountable, flexible, innovative and a good communicator. These translate into being a comforter, an example, a disciplinarian, a friend, a safe space, and a human. If you have more than one child, this is a requirement in multiples and rarely simultaneously.

The same is true as a people leader in the workplace.

The not-for-profit sector challenged me to learn how to navigate individuals in survival mode and contend with there being no such thing as an isolated incident. When the incident is unresolved, and you keep finding yourself reliving the moment, it's looping to teach you a lesson. Physically, I left situations but every occurrence or encounter left unresolved scarred me. People mistreating me made me feel like a bullied 9-year-old. Or a helpless teenager. I would mentally go back to those moments and respond how I should have then.

The detractor in the workplace almost pushed me into retaliation and self-sabotage with their antics. Through self-awareness, coaching, mentorship, and a safe space, I was victorious in that scenario. The trap they set for me failed them. *Do* what you know is right, to the best of your ability. Show up for what is important to you.

Are you learning to do the math? What's the equation?

Accountability + Deciding = Do

Here's how you A.D.D.

Accept Accountability —

Reconcile your issues' origin across a gambit of things.

Decide –

Be intentional about what you want to do with the new revelation.

Do –

Align your actions with your words, thoughts and feelings.

I'm not remotely operating from a place of perfection. It's simply intentionality and awareness. Dots connect every time a scenario feels familiar. I slink back into my version of survival mode when tired, suffering from impostor syndrome and not feeling up to the challenge.

I ask myself about where I've seen these behaviors before, what I did then and ask for help to avoid repetition. Whether it's leading at home, or leading people in the workplace, *I do the math*. This equation has helped me weather all kinds of storms, I hope it can *serve you as well*.

Catherine McNeil
About the Author

As an IO Psychologist and Lean Six Sigma Green Belt, Catherine McNeil is the Principal Consultant of CHBM Services LLC, a holistic career, employee and workforce development consultancy, and the Executive Director of Disruptive INC! Under Catherine's leadership, CHBM Services is the primary for profit funder and partner of Disruptive INC; Disruptive INC reduces poverty among single parents between the ages of 18-40 by providing support via career development and related resources. To date, this organizational partnership has hosted over 20 events, touched over 3,000 households, and raised over $50,000 in corporate, financial, and individual support.

Along with her other accomplishments, Catherine is also the content creator and founder of CHBM Services University, has authored six published parenting-related literary works (available on Amazon) and is the host of the "Let's Chat!" w/ASKCat podcast.

linktr.ee/chbmservices

Chapter 4
Seeing Yourself as a Leader
Integrity Vision & Resilience

*I didn't set out to be a leader.
I didn't dream of being an entrepreneur.
But, I'm so glad I found my way into it anyway.*

By Sierra Melcher

I wore fake glasses for the first year I was a teacher.

I didn't feel like I belonged at the front of the room. I was young and inexperienced. I couldn't see myself in that position of authority. I was only a few years older than my students. So I needed a prop. I needed something that made me look the part and believe the story that I belonged there. It worked, *or so I thought*.

How many ways do we pretend? Because we are in uncharted territory or taking on something new. Because we don't believe in ourselves. We don't see ourselves as leaders or aren't sure how we will get through. How come with fake glasses on *–or real ones–* we can never see ourselves the way others do?

For ages, I kept trying to *be* something, to *be someone*. Looking to others and seeing if I could *pretend* well enough to pull it off: as a teacher, as a business owner, as a parent; SPOILER ALERT, I never felt I ever really pulled it off, *even when I absolutely had.*

Not until I figured out that it was not about copying others, playing a role, or faking it. True leadership came to me over time and it came as much, if not more so, from my struggles and failures as it came from my triumphs. I have been a teacher, a yoga studio owner, and now I am an author and publisher.

In the heart of every great leader lies a profound sense of purpose and an unwavering commitment to guiding their team or audience toward a brighter future. Leadership is a dynamic art that demands the mastery of various traits and skills, but among the foundational pillars that support a leader's journey, three stand out as indispensable: *integrity, vision, and resilience.* This chapter delves into these core attributes that separate good leaders from extraordinary ones.

Becoming a true leader means embodying integrity, vision, and resilience. Hone these three traits to:

- Stay true to who you are and what makes you unique and special or different
- Become able to see, map out, and realize a vision from just an idea
- Learn from your struggles and improve over time; grow with the circumstances into unimaginable possibilities

INTEGRITY

Leading from within means trusting yourself & listening fiercely, having hard conversations, sticking to what you believe in the face of doubt, fear, and possible failure, but doing it anyway, against the odds.

Stay true to yourself. This is much easier said than done, but worth doing. Leading often means finding your own path and blazing your own trail. There aren't always guide posts... but we step forward regardless. Being a visionary requires being honest with yourself. Brave & confident before there is proof.

When I was new to writing, I tried so damn hard to sound smart and impressive. Sincere and insightful. I tried so hard to be a genius. It just didn't work. It was like wearing fake glasses again. I was trying to be who I thought I needed to be, instead of figuring out how to be me in the role.

For ages, I thought authors needed to be a certain way, look a certain way, and write and talk a certain way. Everything I had read supported that belief and so I was trying to fit myself into that mold. The mold didn't fit. I thought there was something wrong with me. Turns out, it was just the wrong mold.

Leadership can feel and sound like a heavy burden. Writing a book and guiding a community can be a lot, but what if it were fun?

So for this reason, when we set out to be a leader, set out to put a vision into place, and set out to guide a community or write a book, our perceptions of that role can often trip us up. I run a successful non-fiction publishing company. I remind our authors that, while they are drafting their books and sharing their expertise, they are becoming authorities and building that credibility through sharing their knowledge through writing. *Author* is the root of the word *authority*. You become an authority by doing the thing; you become a leader by leading.

In life and business, what is okay and not okay is about having and honoring your boundaries. Communicating what feels safe and what feels like betrayal will make all the difference. To be a leader with integrity requires the ability to have hard conversations on all topics. To do this you can't just wear the fake glasses. You need to know you deserve to be there and hold fast to a vision of something better, something worth fighting for.

At Red Thread Publishing, I teach our authors about a really important contradiction. I call it *playful authority*. Far too often we can get bogged down with taking ourselves so seriously that we lose sense of ourselves and the fun that is possible when we grow.

That doesn't mean they need to become a pedantic ass. Rather, quite the opposite is true. Learning to be a playful authority gives you permission to screw it up. Permits you to experiment, learn, and grow. Gives you permission to have fun and be yourself. Authenticity, in all its messy glory, is fundamental to integrity.

Vision

Being a visionary means— seeing something that isn't there. Mapping out and taking steps to craft a new reality makes leadership sound like science fiction. And in some ways, it is metaphysics. It is the ultimate creation act. To have vision as a leader you must also have integrity.

Clarify What You Care About Creating

Leading from within means trusting yourself, and trusting your vision before it manifests. And listening fiercely to that voice that is uniquely yours. It is easy to be swayed to join the crowd, to do what the cool kids are doing, to emulate the people you aspire to be.

In essence, there's nothing wrong with that, but being a visionary requires being honest with yourself, brave, and confident before there's any proof that doing it your way (differently) is worth a try. When you're out on a limb you have to risk, having a vision when you don't have proof of how to get there. You've got to try and by definition, you will fail.

> "What got you here will not get you there."

A couple of times a week I get an email from someone I know, introducing me to someone who wants to write or publish a book. I love to get on calls with strangers with this goal. They have a vision they have yet to fully commit to, a dream that is not yet realized. But when they can see how Red Thread Publishing can make that dream come true, they get turned on. At Red Thread, we're on a mission to support 10,000 women to become successful published authorpreneurs, and thought leaders.

Each day as I speak with a new aspiring author, I am accomplishing my mission: one conversation at a time, I haven't yet accomplished the whole mission. Not all at once. Not today. Not in that one call. But it's enough to help me keep seeing the path and seeing the progress towards the full realization of the goal.

From a vision of my own, I now run a successful international publishing company. I've written 12 books. Now it seems like not a big deal at all. In these calls with aspiring authors, they are trying to test the viability of their vision, to explore if this whisper or calling to write has legs. By taking the time to hear them out, and offer them some guidance and strategy I am not only emboldening their vision, but it furthers our mission: the audacious vision of 10,000 new female authors and thought leaders guiding the next generation.

Vision is a delusion until you make it real. It's impossible until you know how; the way to know how is to try and inevitably screw it up a bunch of times. To be resilient and try again.

Resilience & Reinvention.

CELEBRATE your failures
— "Um, no thanks"

While I longed to be an author, I held myself back for years due to fear and doubt. Then I simply gave up on my dream. It seemed too big, too scary, and too improbable. I was likely to fail. In fact, the statistics nearly guaranteed it... so better not try. I lived like that for half of my adult life.

This is where vision, integrity, and resilience intersect. I had a vision - to write a book. I finally was determined enough to set a goal (publish a book before my daughter's fifth birthday). My integrity made me stick to that promise I made to myself. My resilience allowed me to face my fears of failure and just keep trying till the job was done. Here is a fun hack: "Accelerate growth by being willing to screw it up." I am such a fan of this I wrote an entire book about it, Typo: The Art of Imperfect Creation; give yourself permission to do it badly at first.

Your success directly correlates to your willingness to fail. How good of a leader you are is determined by how clear your vision is and how consistently you can be yourself.

Face down is not a place we aspire to be. But it does not mean we're not going to get there in the process. It's a ripe place for leaders. Face down is a sign of striving; so congratulations. Resilience is what distinguishes leaders who grow from leaders who flail.

Resilience isn't about succeeding or failing at all. You'll do both! Probably lots. Resilience is about not getting stuck in either your struggles or your triumphs. Both can be slippery and dangerous. Resilience is about showing up every day. Holding that vision. Staying true to yourself and being playful as best you can. In that one day, that one meeting, that one exchange. I know when I think about leadership, it comes with all this heavy, long-term responsibility. It drains the fun right out of it. Your willingness to fail defines your success.

Your willingness to fail determines your capacity for success.

What if that was the missing factor, the exact variable you needed to improve?

I was pregnant when I moved to a new city in a foreign country and opened a yoga studio. It sounds crazy now when I write this, but it is what I did. I had no business training or knowledge, I didn't have a business plan or any market research. I just did a thing. It turns out there were several glaring problems right away:

- Who is going to teach the yoga classes in 2 months when I have a newborn?
- How can I afford to hire people to teach before the studio is earning money?

- All the people I can find to teach only speak English, but half of my clientele speak only Spanish.

These were tremendous problems that could have easily closed us down, and nearly did. I am a creative problem solver, so in short order, I had a solution for each problem.

- Hire volunteers recently certified and needing teaching experience – there was a huge market
- Allow them to grow their confidence and their resume – Yoga Internship
- Teach them to speak Spanish – Spanish for Yoga Teachers Language Immersion

These programs turned out to be the most unique and prosperous elements of my yoga studio for years. These creative solutions became what allowed me to sell my business with ease when the time came because I had created a unique value proposition and a huge earning potential that existed nowhere else.

It is not just in my first business that I struggled. It is a pretty reliable factor in business. For this I am grateful.

It is not just having our face-down moments, but owning and sharing them. When I was in my twenties, I would have presented myself as infallible. But that is not true leadership. That is false and fails where people need us the most. I not only made mistakes, I willingly and freely shared them as examples of what not to do and how to do it better next time. Being a leader doesn't require you to be flawless, but rather be willing to make mistakes. Guide others to succeed where you failed. Warn your community about the pitfalls and accelerate the process to not get stuck in the traps where folks get stuck, wasting time and energy.

My company, Red Thread Publishing, is winning awards & accolades. Our authors are having incredible transformations and, more importantly, their books are making a huge impact on the lives of their readers & helping them grow thriving mission-driven and purpose-driven businesses. With every book we have published, I have learned & grown. For every year I have lived, I have had hundreds of failures, missteps, and face-downs. Near quitting moments. But they are just moments. Overwhelm, doubt & fear have been my wrestling partners.

I am grateful for every mistake (and there have been so many), and more to come I am sure.

What if failure was the first step?

What if it were a prerequisite?

Just for fun, here are some leadership pitfalls. Avoid them at all costs. When you find yourself facedown, right in the middle of one, celebrate that you tried.

Leadership pitfalls

- Trying to be someone else, denying yourself
- Doing it like someone else who has been successful
- Following the "I am successful. Do it like me"... NOPE
- Trying to "get it perfect" before implementing an idea
- Hiding your weaknesses & failures at all costs, rather than admitting you're human
- Avoiding hard conversations
- Trying to please/ satisfy everyone

Reflection Questions:

1. If you lead by example by sharing your most disastrous mistakes, how might things change?
2. If you shared your struggles in equal proportion to your success, would your audience doubt you or trust you more?

3. When you are reading someone else's story, what do you appreciate most: about how they have succeeded at all things and how great their life/business is? Or how they messed it up and sorted it out? Who do you find more relatable? More inspirational?

Sierra Melcher
About the Author

Best-selling author, international speaker & educator, Sierra Melcher is the founder of **Red Thread Publishing LLC.** She leads an all-female publishing company, with a mission to support 10,000 women to become successful published authors & thought leaders. Offering world-class coaching & courses that focus on community, collaboration, and a uniquely feminine approach at every stage of the authoring process.

Sierra has a Master's degree in education and has spoken & taught around the world. Originally from the United States, Sierra lives in Medellin, Colombia with her daughter.

Sierra Melcher is the author of 14 books to date.
amazon.com/author/sierramelcher

linktr.ee/redthreadpublishing
www.redthreadbooks.com

- instagram.com/redthreadbooks
- linkedin.com/in/sierra-melcher
- amazon.com/author/sierramelcher
- goodreads.com/sierra-melcher

Chapter 5
Six Steps to Connecting with Folks
Having Courageous and Crucial Conversations

By Gloria Cotton

Have you ever needed to have a serious conversation with someone and just thinking about it raised your anxiety and stress levels? Ever keep putting it off and putting it off until you realize you no longer "needed" to have it, now you "had" to. Ever feel your anxieties and stressors (and probably those of others too!) increasing to the point that more and more people, performances and perhaps even brands were being negatively impacted? Ever been concerned about another shoe falling or stuff hitting the fan and it NOT being a pretty sight? Ever wish and hope, think and pray the whole thing would just magically go away or that someone else would do it – even though you knew you were the best and maybe the only person who could and should?

Well, if you've ever felt any of these things, welcome to the club! You are not alone.

My Goal: As a Strategic Diversity, Equity & Inclusion (DEI) Executive Consultant and Pro-inclusionist, I wanted to reduce and maybe even prevent anxiety and stress that I and anyone else might be feeling about being courageous enough to have crucial conversations in optimal and transformative ways. When I looked at times I'd been successful, I discovered some common themes: whatever we were discussing, each person felt safe physically, emotionally, mentally, and psychologically. We created that safety by working together to make sure everyone understood what we all needed to feel welcome, valued, respected, heard, understood, and supported when we agreed and when we disagreed when the answer was "yes" and when it was "no." The yield from all that work allowed us to be able to:

- **Be** confident that, as human beings and as professionals – no matter our age, how long we'd worked together or known each other, whatever similarities and differences of our dynamic and delicious diversity, we had grown together. We worked well together. And when we didn't or when it was hard, we trusted each other, gave each other grace, and worked through the bumps in the road – together.
- **Know** the real "pain points" and what we all need to acknowledge that would eliminate and replace the pain and need. Yeah. We also felt safe enough to discuss historic, current, personal, professional, and cultural things that had or might sabotage our efforts and intentions in small to great ways.
- **Have** a clear understanding of what was needed, the gaps, who/what would be impacted if we were successful and if we were not, and the roles and responsibilities of each person.
- **Do** what was necessary to initially and ongoingly approach each other and the topic with uncompromised respectful curiosity, willingness, openness, growth mindsets, and commitments to hold ourselves and each other accountable.

The Tool: When I was working with folks I had known, respected, and loved for years, it was no problem. We had grown and matured together and created our behavioral guidelines and rules of engagement over time. It was fabulous. We had the healed battle scars to prove that we'd done it together. But there were times when I wasn't working with my long-term friends. Often teams would be put together and we'd have to *storm, norm, and perform* quickly. Most of the time we were expected to jump straight to performing, with no time to peel back our onion bulbs to storm and norm. But I knew the connections and comforts built during those two phases had to happen. Otherwise, we still might perform with excellence, but with more difficulty and, frankly, not with as much fun!

So, I developed a 6-step process that I hoped would help new team members connect with each other and have our "Be, Know, Have, Do" answers quickly. The model represented the key behaviors and skills that I and my long-standing team members had used, a process that helped us see, hear, and experience each other as advocates and allies vs. adversaries or combatants.

Here's what I came up with:

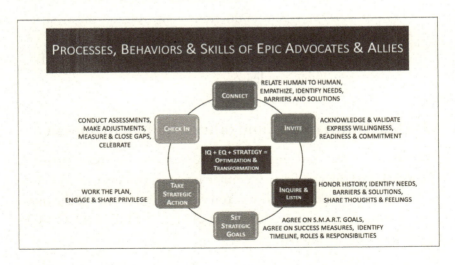

Doing the Work:

- First, go through the first step (Connect) focused only on yourself. This may take some time and you may need a coach to help you identify and acknowledge things from your past and present as well as your aspirational goals, influencers, concerns, and triggers.
- Next, go through all 6 steps with both you and your other team member(s) in mind.
- To be most successful, be open to applying whatever step is needed. In other words, using this process isn't about checking the box. As people and things are added or changed, revisit it. Be fluid and in flow with what's needed to get the best outcome given new or changing information or understanding.
- Of course, you may use the questions I've noted below. Or, if you prefer, use the ones I've included to help you create your own list of questions.
- **CAUTION:** You won't have all the answers for the other team member(s) when you're working alone. Even if you think you know them well (and even if you do), be open to learning new or different things. One of the most dangerous things about working with others is thinking that everything we know or have learned about them is all there is to know and learn.

CONNECT with myself and others, human to human

NOTE: First ask and answer these questions for/about yourself. Then ask and answer from the other person's perspective. *What do you think their responses will be?* You can ask them some of the questions during your conversation. (NOT ALL OF THEM AT ONCE. It can seem like an interrogation.)

- What do I know about the issue and the person?
- What do I need to do so that I feel safe before, during, and after the conversation physically, emotionally, intellectually, mentally, and psychologically?
- What is my perception and perspective about what happened in the past? What's happening now?
- What are the impacts on relational performance (who) and task performance (what, when, how) as well as the overall culture?
- What assumptions am I making?

NOTE: I've learned to ask myself, "What assumptions am I making?" versus "Am I making assumptions?" We all make assumptions, consciously and unconsciously. We all have conscious and unconscious biases, both positive and negative. That doesn't make us good or bad people. It just makes us people! Engage someone else to help you discover the assumptions you might be making and the biases that may be influencing you. Ask them for feedback regarding their observations. You might ask when/if they noticed the possibility of your biases influencing your behavior, e.g., overspeaking someone during a meeting, not including the name of a key stakeholder on a document distribution list, etc.

- How does this issue align with the mission, vision, values, and strategic goal of the organization? What is or can be compromised and how does that impact our brand?
- Why do I care? What do I win/lose if I do/don't address this and achieve a positive outcome? What's my WIIFM (What's In It For Me), my inspiration and motivation?
- What are the consequences (positive and negative) of addressing this? What are the consequences (positive and negative) of *not* addressing it?
- What are my personal and professional barriers and triggers?

- What are the things that could cause me to shut down and shut the other person out?
- Would I think and feel differently if it was about a different issue or involving a different person?
- Can I connect with the other person's experience whether I've had a similar experience or not? Do I want to? NOTE: This is what empathy is about, y'all!
- Am I willing to work to create equitable solutions with this person?
- Who else needs to be involved?

"[The pandemic] has magnified the need for us all to connect as human beings before we connect as co-workers, business partners, etc. We're social animals. At any level of an organization, if you know your leader and teammates care about you beyond that day's performance, it's more fun and fulfilling to serve a shared deeper purpose. Leaders who intentionally build in those extra minutes in meetings to hear people out, offer comfort or advice, and even leave space for laughter and occasional nonsense, are ultimately building a more resilient team."

— *John Jacobs*, Cofounder and Chief Creative Optimist of *Life is Good*

INVITE key players/users and developers/contributors

- Why should/shouldn't I accept my invitation to have a conversation about this?
- What's in it for me and others to leverage personal and professional time, privilege, and other resources now?
- What is my motivation/inspiration? Why is this issue important to me?
- How will I keep myself inspired and motivated?

- What will make a positive difference to me personally, to others, to the culture, to the products and services that we give others?

"The people you are leading have big expectations of you. They want you to be perfect and often forget that you are human. But the more human you are with them, the more trust and empathy they lend to you. They understand you better. That gives you the ability to do so much more, as people give you the benefit of the doubt."

— *Alain Bejjani*, CEO of Majid Al Futtaim Group

INQUIRE & LISTEN to stories, thoughts, feelings, and needs with respectful curiosity

- What's the bottom line?
- What's the range and impacts of acceptable to ideal outcome(s)?
- What's been done already and when? What worked, what failed, and why? Think about people, processes, procedures, and past and present culture. Consider influences of the external culture also.
- What are the pain and pleasure points? Sometimes there are varying degrees of wins and losses. Are these things known, acknowledged, and factored into next-step decision-making?
- How, when, and by whom should measurable steps be taken?
- Has each person felt safe enough and had time to react and respond?
- Have all voices been heard?
- Acknowledge there will be stumbles and fumbles. Important benefits of using this process are people often

become more comfortable sharing information, getting to know each other, and building meaningful connections and trust. Interestingly, along with the growth of these things also comes the willingness to give each other grace, to cut each other some slack when stumbles and fumbles occur.
- What is the aligned strategic action plan? What are each person's responsibilities and accountabilities?
- What can get in the way of our success? Consider the impact of position and personal power and the privileges, habits, and blind spots that go along with them.

Bottom line: The information you can gather when people feel safe enough to share their truths from both IQ and EQ is priceless. *Let me restate the importance of people knowing and feeling that they are welcome, valued, respected, heard, understood, and strategically supported.* I've been in too many meetings where people have talked around the real issues and talked about talking about what they need to really talk about. Effective leaders invest in relationships where people can breathe and don't have to walk on eggshells to not only get the job done, but to make sure it's done while optimizing people, products, and services.

> *"In the 21st century, more than ever before, effective leadership is about serving others. The Digital Revolution is transforming a transaction-based world into a relationship-based world. The capacity of individuals and organizations to serve others is greater than ever before. You're able to create more relationships, and serve more people more effectively in those relationships, than even our recent predecessors could have conceived."*
>
> *— James Strock, Author and Speaker*

SET STRATEGIC GOALS – align the needs of the people and the needs of the organization

They should strengthen and optimize targeted tasks and relational performance.

- What is the ideal goal? What do I/we/the organization want and need short-, mid- and long-term?
- It's OK to go beyond this specific issue and need. But remember to clearly address their current need. Too often people begin to look at possible organizational impacts and diminish or ignore the original reason for conversation. Often, they move on to something else and never get back to addressing the original need.
- Make sure you collaboratively identify roles and responsibilities for both of you and be honest about what you can and can't do.
- Identify other people and things that may need to be secured, if possible. If you don't have them and can't get them, be real about it!
- Collaboratively develop goals and tactics that are ideal – meeting all specified needs or acceptable though not ideal. Keep this in mind when either the culture or the people are resistant.
- Make sure the goals serve and are directly or indirectly aligned with the what and why of the mission/vision, the who and how of the values and current and future aspirations, be S.M.A.R.T. (Specific, Measurable, Achievable, Relevant, and Timely), and relevant to each person, role, and location so that everyone knows and can tell anyone why the goal(s) are important to them personally and professionally and how they help make the organization a success.

Bottom line: Strategic goals should meet and align individual, team, and organizational needs in ways that inspire people, their willingness and engagement, whatever their role.

"One of the criticisms I've faced over the years is that I'm not aggressive enough or assertive enough or maybe somehow because I'm empathetic, it means I'm weak. I totally rebel against that. I refuse to believe that you cannot be both compassionate and strong."

— Jacinda Ardern, Prime Minister of New Zealand

TAKE STRATEGIC ACTION –

It is important that we talk the talk. It is equally important for us to walk the walk.

- It's about show and tell. Not just tell.
- Now that you have your collaborative Strategic Plan, bring it to life. Time to activate it.
- Make sure everyone is clear about timelines, roles and responsibilities, measurements, and check-ins.
- Leverage and share the relevant privileges of all involved.

Bottom line: Even when we plan and say all the right things and communicate those things, people and organizations need people to make those strategic plans realities for everyone. We have to deliver on our promises for our human and organizational safety, health, and well-being.

"Vision without action is merely a dream. Action without vision just passes the time. Vision with action can change the world."

— Joel Barker, Futurist, Author, Lecturer, Advertising Executive, and the first person to popularize the concept of paradigm shifts in the corporate world.

CHECK-IN – Conduct strategically planned, needs-based, and impromptu check-ins with key players and people who are doing the work and end users.

- Be careful to appropriately include the person who brought the issue to your attention.
- Pay attention and welcome input and feedback from both yay-sayers and nay-sayers. All the micro- and macro-level data will help you continue to optimize excellence.
- Remember and assess data of both internal and external customers to determine their experiences, needs, loyalty, what they admire about your competitors, etc.

Bottom line: While we want to celebrate successes of the past and continue to learn from them, at the same time, acknowledge (not celebrate) and learn from failures and raise the standard of excellence. Set and deliver on new levels of excellence in every aspect of our business.

"Strategy is not linear. Most often, it is circular. It means that a company's strategy changes as it progresses rather than progressing in a straight line. A circular strategy is more effective because it allows feedback loops to be maintained, and quick adjustments are possible."

— *Ernst Friedrich "Fritz" Shoemaker, Architect, economic thinker, statistician, and economist.*

The Wrap-Up

The 6-Step process I presented in this chapter has helped me and my team members to connect and work better with each other. As a bonus, we procrastinate less because we aren't afraid to confront issues. So things don't turn into big, hairy bodacious beasts. In fact, I look forward to and am energized thinking about having those courageous, crucial conversations that I used to put off and have anxiety and stress about. I hope it helps you too!

Gloria Cotton
About the Author

Gloria (Glo) Cotton is an Executive DEI Leadership Consultant and "Pro-inclusionist." For more than 30 years she has worked with leaders and team members at all levels within corporations, government agencies, community organizations, and families across the USA and globally.

Glo says, "We must keep strategic goals top of mind. I help people do that and build skills and practices so they connect with each other as human beings at the same time. It's not always easy. An added complexity now is that more people are working virtually and experiencing physical as well as social distancing. One of the benefits of building those connections so we _know_ each other rather than just _knowing about_ each other is that we don't feel we have to constantly walk on eggshells. We can be human, foibles and all, and still have fewer misunderstandings or concern for anyone's physical, emotional, mental, or psychological safety. That's something most people want. I help them build and strengthen their practices and skills so they can grow their human and cultural competence ... and have some fun along the way."

linktr.ee/GloriaCotton

Chapter 6
When Leading a Family Business
How To Honor The Past, Optimize The Present, & Change For The Future

By Dan Gershenson

If you're the leader of a family business who wants to honor the past, optimize the present, and be ready for change in the future, you're about to discover how to bring a new level of purpose and performance to your life's work by transforming every possible interaction your most ideal customers will ever have with you.

I've never been good with the phrase, *"This is the way we've always done it."* I'm a person who always wants to have his own stamp on a business and leave my mark. I don't want my impact to be minor and forgettable as a historical footnote. Why? To my knowledge, we get to live this life that we only have one of. And I'm not living it to merely be the caretaker of someone else's legacy.

I suppose that's why I've now spent most of my professional life as a business owner. But it wasn't originally designed to be this way.

Eight years into my career, I was perfectly happy working as a Copywriter in what I considered my "dream job," a large advertising agency in downtown Chicago. I'd been with the agency for a few years and had a grand vision of working there for the rest of my professional days (never mind that the advertising industry is notorious for high turnover).

I always admired how my dad had worked one job for his entire career, steadily moving up the ladder to a position of authority and great respect from others across nearly 40 years. From my perspective, his impact on the business seemed to be nothing short of legendary. There were so many vital points where he had a profound impact, saving and making his company millions of dollars. All the while, he was a trusted source who always had the ear of the CEO.

There was so much for me to emulate from that path. I felt I was well on my way, too. I had just broken through a lot of internal red tape to come up with some ideas with my design partner, Jeff, that were literally ready for prime time. It was for our client, one of the most prominent insurance brands in the world. Insurance wasn't "sexy" compared to writing for beer, athletic shoes, or automobiles. But I was proud of the story we were telling and our ads for the client landed on national television, radio, and big publications in print. I couldn't wait to show my wife, parents, and grandmother the fruits of my hard labor.

When I finally saw my work out in the world, I felt like, *"This is it. This is where I make a name for myself. I'm going to be moving up in this agency. Look out, universe."*

I felt this with great conviction because my parents always told me, *"As long as you work hard and do your best, everything will work out."*

I was on top of the mountain. And then I fell all the way to the bottom.

Soon after my work was publicized in front of millions of eyeballs, I was laid off from the agency. The client was cutting back their business and I was a casualty.

I'll never really know why it was me and not someone else. All I know is it was one of the most soul-crushing days of my life. It is for anyone who experiences this. You go to your boss in tears. You go to HR feeling numb. You must pack up your office, quickly say goodbye to friends you've made, and leave the building.

I didn't get to have the impact and leave the legacy I wanted to make for myself.

Looking back on that moment, my entire trajectory in life changed. I thought all my aspirations and dreams were dead. I thought what my parents told me was a lie. I thought I would never find my purpose again.

Just two years later, I would become a business owner with two other partners, ambitiously and somewhat naively running an advertising agency. When we closed that agency five and a half years later, all of that self-doubt and feeling lost in the wilderness started to flood back.

But this time, something was different.

In losing a business and not just a job, I should have been devastated but, for some reason, I found myself more determined than ever to ensure what I was experiencing wouldn't happen to others. Because it just didn't have to.

I knew the challenge of wearing many different hats in my roles, even growing into some of those hats.

I felt the emotion of victory in winning new pieces of business and growing revenue to new heights.

I understood the roller coaster of forces you couldn't always control, such as the economy or a client going out of business.

I was plenty familiar with shiny objects in the way of tools and technologies that always seemed to promise a shortcut to prosperity but couldn't live up to it.

And I had the same feelings of frustration and despair that came with throwing new ideas against the wall, hoping that just one of them would stick.

All of this was combining to send me a message that, even though I would be beginning a new chapter and had no idea at the time what that would look like, my work with business owners wasn't done. Not by a long shot.

These leaders wanted to evolve their well-established companies for the present day while honoring the past foundation built by those who came before them. In doing so, they would be better positioned to make positive changes for the future.

Now that I knew what these feelings entailed, I promised to dedicate myself to rescuing other business owners who felt lost in a constant sea of questions and complexity. I would find ways to pull them out of that abyss so they could make critical marketing decisions with supreme confidence and clarity.

But *who and where were these people exactly?* And *how* would I know I could help them if I saw and heard them?

Find Your Ideal Client

As both a brand director and business owner, I found myself uniquely qualified as a person who could help other business owners who didn't want to sit still and rest on their laurels.

I could see the ideal leader I wanted to help most: The second generation leader of a family business.

I didn't merely list basic information about this individual. I pictured them as flesh and blood going about their day, with all the challenges that came with it.

These folks are frequently caught between honoring a mother or father who started the business and where they want to go to have their own legacy. So they have a bit of an inherent drama of where they are right now – honoring the past while optimizing the present.

Why do less than 10% of family businesses survive past the second or third generation of owners? It might be because the next generation is constantly caught between honoring the past, optimizing the present, and being driven by change in the future.

I am fascinated by someone looking to make a change or evolve the business that they've been handed, which is a fantastic opportunity. Not many of us get to hit the ground running like that with something already established for us.

Yet, they also have a unique challenge that we don't have. Family businesses in their second generation are not just starting from the ground up with nothing to refer back to.

They can't simply say, *"Well, screw everything that happened in the past. I'm following my path."* Because that will cause significant problems within their own family personally, they must make at least some kind of nod to what they've been given, which is a gift.

At the same time, they cannot live this life as only a legacy caretaker. They're trying to tell their own story that somebody in the future can appreciate.

What appeals to me is that these people want to make a change and are not just continuing the same thing because I don't believe that people who operate in the status quo are living.

On a deeper level, I believe:

Everybody deserves to have their own story written for themselves and not live someone else's story.

This Is How It's Supposed To Feel

Seeing your ideal client in your mind's eye is one thing. But you won't absolutely know who you want to serve most until you experience the feeling of doing so in the real world.

That's what happened to me. Out of the blue, I received a phone call from a former client, a family business I had worked with nearly a decade ago.

The only problem was that while I was working with them, I was freelancing for the agency that handled their account. And when I started my own agency again, I had to part company with all of those clients I'd helped for someone else.

Now, nine years later, they called with some news: they'd fired the old agency I worked for and said, *"You know, we've never loved working with someone from a writing standpoint as much as we loved working with you."*

Of course, I was over the moon at this development, but that wasn't the turning point to know they were the ideal client.

The turning point was when I came to their office. In the nine years since we last talked, their company, established over several decades, had grown exponentially. They were making over $30 million in revenue with about 75 employees and plans to build another building next to the two they already had.

Life couldn't be better for them, right?

You would think so. Except I sat down and the first two words out of their mouths were, *"Help us."*

Help them? They were doing fantastic, growing, and having a wonderful year!

Not necessarily in their eyes, however. They were frustrated about how to tell their story from a marketing perspective. They didn't know which strategies and initiatives to pursue. They didn't know how to optimize for the present, even as they were caught between honoring the legacy of the previous generation of owners while thinking about making changes for the future.

That's when it hit me: *They were just like me!* They didn't want just to be doing the same things or being mere brand caretakers either. They wanted the company to have its best year ever by embracing who it needed to become.

I hadn't seen it before, but I aligned with this second-generation business owner. It was giving me an opportunity. I never considered that a company that looked like such a smooth, well-oiled machine from the outside could be so challenged by marketing strategy and execution.

I told myself, *"I can help people like this continue a legacy, which is different than saying I can help them make an extra couple million dollars."*

I'm an extremely emotional person when it comes to relationships. I crave them so much that I appreciate when leaders truly see their people as family. They feel a huge responsibility to their employees (and their households) in a way I've rarely seen.

I have always wanted to be part of a company that felt like family and, when you can at least work with the next generation of a true family business, that's something special.

After only a few months of working with this client, I said the one thing that made me know I had finally seen my ideal client: *"If I had ten more like these, I would be loving life."*

This emotion spoke to me in a way that a different kind of client would not. I was inspired by them wanting to make a real difference long-term for their family business and I would do everything in my power to help them experience that.

One powerful thought awakened my soul from within in thinking about working with the best client: It's not a needle in a haystack or an experience to enjoy once every decade. Why wouldn't we want to at least try to target those people the most all the time?

After all, if we know what the ideal client looks like, behaves like, is challenged by, and is excited by, why should we actively target customers who are anything less? Those people will filter in anyway, but they're not the best. Are they? Everybody in the company should know what they look like if they're the best. Everybody in the company should be on board with targeting them first and foremost.

I'm not saying to refuse customers who aren't ideal. But consider this about your potential customers: Who are the best and *why* are they the best? Not just because they pay you the most but because they make you feel the best about what you do.

They will give you good, qualified referrals. They will provide you with a five-star review. With that combination alone, why not strive for that every single time? Why not tailor everything you have towards that kind of client?

Shift towards that.

Evolve For The Journey

For many years, I worked with businesses that felt the journey to new customers was as easy as advertising on TV or radio. Or perhaps putting an ad in a paper or sending direct mail.

The Internet, social media, and artificial intelligence have changed all that to give business owners a kind of power, unlike anything they've experienced before. How? No longer is it a sure thing that he who wins customers is the one with the most money and resources. Now, it's a safe bet that he who wins customers is one with a superb understanding of the journey his potential next buyer is on. I'm talking about every possible point to connect with that prospective customer in a natural, not sales-ish way.

Here's what I mean:

If you're selling a complex service, never are you going to have somebody just walk into your office and say, "*I want one of those.*" People are more complicated in some ways. And in other ways, they're simple because they *just want to be led to the next stage.* Especially if you offer a service that could cost hundreds, thousands, or millions of dollars at a time.

It could take serious interaction with your business for them to say: "*This is right for me.*" It's going to first take them knowing and liking you. But that's not enough. They'll then need to pivot and say, "*OK. I'll put you on a short list because I trust a good portion of what you're saying.*"

Don't get too excited and call it a done deal. They're not buying yet.

That said, you could go a long way toward that purchase or signed engagement if you execute on the <u>one</u> part that is almost always missed during the prospective buyer's journey: *Are you giving them something to try before they can buy so they feel comfortable utilizing your service?*

Even when they ultimately buy, are you doing something in those first 30 days that really reinforces their investment so they don't have buyer's remorse?

This is usually the point where people say, *"OK! That's a sale. We've done good. On to the next one."*

Hold on. Let me provide food for thought: They bought *one* service, yes. But why can't they buy *two* or *three* services? Why can't they refer you to another well-qualified company that might need your services?

These *repeat* and *refer* stages are frequently under-nurtured, if not forgotten about completely.

See, people aren't going to engage your services after seeing your brand one time. You can't post on social media once or send out an eNewsletter once and expect someone to call your office, ready to start working with you.

That's just not going to happen. If it happens once, I'll be amazed. It's not going to happen twice.

So, realize that because your sale is complex, you must have a certain degree of patience with each stage of the buyer's journey to a relationship with you: From knowing and liking your proposition to trusting and trying it for the first time. And beyond.

It also serves as an excellent way to identify where communication gaps occur. For example, if they know and like your company enough to visit your website but do not trust you enough to try a demo, why is that? There has to be a reason.

This mindset moves owners from honoring the legacy of the past to taking careful steps toward optimizing for the present. It's also a real framework for why people buy and what we can do to communicate in each stage, even anticipating the questions they may have in each stage that we can answer.

In thinking about every stage with such intentionality, you can radically transform every interaction your ideal customers will ever have with you.

Continually done well, it can even build and strengthen relationships that last for generations.

Dan Gershenson
About the Author

Dan Gershenson of Caliber Brand Strategy + Content Marketing is one of Chicago's highest-rated Fractional Chief Marketing Officers (CMO), helping multi-generational business owners clarify and expand their brands to attract and retain higher-paying clients. Dan specializes in brand strategy, content, SEO, social media, e-marketing, and new business development. He has been in the advertising and marketing space for nearly 30 years, frequently speaking on the subjects of marketing strategy, social selling, entrepreneurialism, and reputation management. He is the co-author of the best-selling book, "<u>Content Marketing for Local Search: Create Content that Google Loves & Prospects Devour</u>."

Chapter 7
Lead From Within
Your Company, Your Industry, & Yourself

By Joy Poli

Feeling Valued as an Employee

I was led down the hall of my office building by the Office Manager, carrying a heavy, and mildly embarrassing, mother's pumping bag...*if you know, you know.*

I reflected on a conversation I had a few weeks prior with my male supervisor. He asked what I needed to make my transition back to work seamless (after FMLA for my second child, but my first post-child birthing experience in "Corporate America"). I'm not going to lie; it was an awkward conversation and I remember my sheepish inquiry about a mother's room. Those who know me know I'm not a shy person, but this felt like a very personal conversation and an uncomfortable request to have to make to my male superior. He informed me I was the first to ask and that he'd see what they could accommodate. Right before my return, he let me know that he was able to get me what I needed. I was excited to see what they had done as I had been hearing of other companies doing amazing things for working mothers' rooms.

The Office Manager jingled her keys, handing me a spare one that she took off the keychain. "This is for you" she said, using a different one to unlock the door. She turned the knob, I waited in breathless anticipation with a little excitement bubbling to the surface as she swung open the door. I stood there - motionless. There it was, in all of its glory - a dusty, dirty, tiny closet with a single chair facing a large wire shelving unit. "It locks," she says as if trying to reassure me. She continues "only you and I have the key." I blinked, staring at the giant shelving units' slats wondering to myself "How can I use this?" Things would most definitely fall through the slats. For those of you who don't know, breast pumps are not made up of large parts. There are a lot of pieces to assemble and disassemble in what is supposed to be done in the most sanitary space possible. Pretty much every part of a pump needs to be sanitized immediately after each use. That's why making your employee pump in the bathroom is a ridiculous notion and, a few years prior, it had just started to gain momentum as being frowned upon; news stories regarding changes were everywhere as of late. I mean when you think about the reasons behind this wave of demand for better pumping conditions, it makes complete logical sense; we're talking about unsanitary conditions being offered for basic working mother's needs. Working mothers were fed up, and rightfully so. What kind of message does that give them about their value as an employee?

We both stood there, in the doorway of this tiny closet. I turned to her, confused and frustrated, and said "Ummmm....I don't think this is going to work." "Why?" she asked curtly. Her tone made it clear she thought I was being difficult. She was "in charge" of the office, or that's how she saw it. Many took issue with that, but she was protected as she was the direct admin to the biggest player in the building, and those who challenged her lost. I naively arrived that day thinking there would be someone who made sure I had everything I needed to ensure a smooth transition back into the workforce. Boy, was I wrong. Her reputation didn't matter to me. This felt like lackluster effort, at best. I had to say something - this simply wasn't acceptable.

Self- Advocacy

I cleared my throat, took a breath, and responded "I need a table of some sort to put things on." I gestured to a room that clearly had nothing that could be used. I squirmed at the thought of having to give more detail on something so personal, again, and continued by saying "and...an outlet so I can plug in...," I said trailing off.

It became crystal clear to me that, although my supervisor did his best to communicate my needs from afar (he lived and worked remotely), followed through on the specifics (where the room was, who had access, what the room looked like, what the room had in it, etc.), that it was nearly impossible to prepare for my return as someone who didn't have the knowledge to understand my needs as a working mother.

I was still reeling in shock. I couldn't believe it. I worked for a Billion Dollar award-winning organization; the Corporate office filled with young, vibrant, energetic, and talented staff. How could I be the first? *Why weren't they more aware? Where was the follow through?*

As the Company's HR Leader, I was tasked with hiring top talent on a daily basis for this company. I knew about the perks being given to entice the best of the best to come and work for us, as I was the one who was negotiating their offers on the Company's behalf. The Company spared no dollar there. But then I face this?!? (Imagine me gesturing to the room.) It didn't make sense to me. It didn't align with the company's external brand and their internal core values. It certainly didn't make me feel great as their employee.

The Office Manager stared at me for a second, blinking, thinking, blinking, and then took action, asking me to wait in the hall for a minute as she made a few hurried trips back and forth from the mother's room to another room. Her final act was to lay an extension cord from that room through the hallway and into the mother's room. "Ok!" she sighed breathlessly in an accomplished tone, opening the door wide to show me what she had done. She had cleared off a shelf about chair-high and laid about 5 of the moving boxes flat on the shelving unit to act as a table. She pointed to it saying, "There's your table and plug" and walked away without another word.

I stood there for a moment, stunned, feeling so much frustration that tears began to fill my eyes; I quickly closed the door before I lost my composure. At this point, I just wanted to get this over with and regroup with my supervisor. I set up and sat down. My head was spinning and I thought to myself: *"How is this better than the bathroom? Is this really how industry leaders treat their employees?"* I couldn't believe it.

I thought *"Is this the best we can do for our employees? If this is how the company is treating me, how are they treating others, who have less seniority, and don't know their rights as an employee?"*

We Needed to do Better

We needed to *be* better. You can't just say you're an industry leader; you actually have to lead by example. After all, if we were tasked with recruiting high-level employees (which included working parents) at the top of their sales game, then we should have the best internal resources and support available to our employees, providing more than just the bare minimum legal requirements.

This wasn't a small company hurting for revenue. It's not like we didn't have the resources necessary to make the room more than just bare bones. Where was the effort to show care, thoughtfulness, and consideration beyond the basics? I took this as my *Opportunity to Champion* for our employees as my role as a leader in HR is to advocate for all employees, and to speak up for them so they don't have to.

HR is as integral to a business as sales, marketing, finance, and legal. HR leaders are tasked with *aligning HR and business goals/strategy* to produce optimal business outcomes and create a connection between employee and business success by setting clear expectations. HR should be seen as stakeholders and Business Partners. After all, it's HR's role to think about the entire employee experience.

Thank goodness I had enough experience to know it was time to advocate for myself and others in the office who would follow after me. I made it my mission as the company's HR Leader to do right by our mothers returning to work. A series of upgrades were made to the room because I spoke up for the betterment of the organization and its employees.

Advocating for Others

But why do I care? Well, as someone who was severely bullied in grade school and had real-life Forrest Gump's "seat's taken" experiences on the daily, I know what it feels like to not be able to advocate for yourself. Advocacy for others has been a part of my job since interning in college for a women's and children's Domestic Violence shelter while obtaining my Bachelor's in Criminology and Law from Marquette University in Milwaukee, Wisconsin. That combination, along with my childhood, drew me to how rules, regulations, and laws worked, why/how they were created, and who they were created for. I believed in "just and right" since I had been wronged for so long.

After graduation, I worked the first 5 years of my career as an advocate in the Felony Cook County court system for victims & witnesses of crimes in Chicagoland. I strengthened the muscle of advocacy every day in court, supporting people through the worst experiences of their lives. I held their hands through things like baby autopsies, pictures and testimonies of loved ones, heartbreaking news, and being someone to lean on during a time of real pain (which no person should ever have to endure).

My passion for speaking up for those who couldn't speak for themselves was sparked in college. It became a full flame as I sat through criminal court, case after case, I listened while people relived the worst experiences of their lives. I saw the worst parts of humanity, and it made me curious; I wanted to understand *what* makes people tick. I really enjoyed analyzing the human behavior behind it all.

Throughout my career as an advocate both in the justice system, Corporate America, and the small to medium business space, I've made it my mission to be an inclusive leader: to make sure all voices are heard and all have a seat at the table. Over my career, I've been described as many things: *"Tenacious* with a T", "Pleasantly Persistent", and even a "Bulldog." I think you can see, I'm one determined person. I attribute that characteristic to my life experiences.

I left my corporate position to start my own HR Advisory Firm over 8 years ago. At Strategic Talent Resources, *I help business owners and their leaders show up as the best version of themselves daily in order to attract and retain top talent*. We help growing companies with all things recruiting and retention related - aiding in the creation of a structurally sound company with a inviting culture necessary to sustain consistent retention of Top Talent. We work with business leaders who want to challenge their own narratives and show up as their best selves consistently to contribute to a healthy, thriving, enjoyable company culture where their employees feel appreciated regularly and have an equitable seat at the table.

That means I have the conversations nobody likes to have, but the conversations that need to be had in order to make sure these conversations are handled with care and consideration for all involved. For the sake of the company, its brand, its culture, its leaders, and its employees.

After 20 years working in HR as a leader, I know how detrimental it can be to an organization to have the wrong person in a leadership role within your company. I find it so important to have tough conversations with leaders, challenging them to show up as their best selves every day, doing the work needed to have the best leadership skills necessary to run a thriving business with a valued workforce.

The Importance of Good Leaders

Without the right leaders, long-term revenue growth and retention are not sustainable. For example, I worked with a company that had two leaders within the same department, both with their own teams doing the same jobs, but with completely different outcomes. Additionally, both leaders had the same job openings on their teams, but each leader was different in their leadership styles. One was proudly a micromanager, and the other gave near complete autonomy to their team and focused on metrics to determine performance success and growth opportunities. They each handled obstacles and decision-making differently. One utilized their leaders as a group of trusted advisers to themselves, and the other made decisions that were often questioned by all on his team. When it came to job openings on their teams, the micromanager had many openings that were difficult to find internal applicants for, as everyone knew his reputation, and employee applicant referrals, of course, weren't regularly flowing in for this same reason. Meanwhile, the other leader always had candidates reaching out to him asking if there were any openings on his team. Ultimately, it came down to the fact that the micromanager didn't inspire people to perform. There was no drive internally that was contagious. There was no excitement, clarity or communication. There was no directive, direction, or guidance offered. It was mass confusion. It was dog eat dog. It was every person out for themselves. It was apparent enough that one day the leader with less interest from applicants when it came to his job openings came to me and asked why so many applicants were interviewing for his peer's opening when none were signed up for interviews with him.

I had two choices. I could be honest with him, knowing it would most likely make him uncomfortable and/or possibly fall on deaf ears as he didn't seem the type to take constructive feedback well, or I could tell him that I have no idea why. I tried the honest approach, but he wasn't interested in making the changes I suggested. Instead, he kept adjusting what he was looking for in a candidate, almost on a consistent basis, instead of adjusting his perspective and molding himself into a leader that people would want to work for and with.

Did he *really* care about why no one wanted to work for him? No. He told me the only reason it concerned him was because it affected his income as a sales leader. He decided not to change his own narrative and it's impossible to fix a problem when you deny one exists. Needless to say, not much changed for him because he wasn't willing to make the changes necessary to have top producers on his team. He didn't give existing employees the opportunity to grow because he wasn't willing to put in the work himself. Which made me sad to see but nothing I could say as his HR Leader would change his fixed mindset. The issue was the candidates and never his own. It was a shame and something that stuck with me all of these years. If only he truly cared, his impact could have been mighty. What a shame indeed.

It was at that moment I decided that I only wanted to work with business owners and company leaders who cared to show up as the best version of themselves, inspiring others to do the same. I knew this was something I had to do not only because of my desire to work with employers who care, but also because there is a workforce movement happening. One you may be aware of, or possibly not, but regardless it's still happening.

Evolution or Stagnation

Back when I started in the workforce, there were a million and one webinars, articles, news stories, and more about how to work with Millennials. We were talked about like we were a group that was difficult to understand and a handful to deal with when all we were doing was challenging the systems built long ago and expecting evolution based on the current times as nothing is meant to last forever as is.

Now we have generations after us doing that and more, and they're not tolerating the excuse of "that's just the way it is." They'll bounce by "ghosting" and "quiet quitting" because ultimately the workforce mentality has changed from needing to wanting.

Fair and equitable pay are table stakes and no longer a "perk" of being your employee. Employees want to be inspired by their leaders; they want pay transparency; they want to be a part of the bigger picture. Top Talent is attracted to those at the top of their game.

Great Leadership

Inspiring and leading others isn't as hard as you think it is as long as you're willing to put in the work. In order to truly inspire and lead others, you must first understand that true leaders don't inspire by telling, they inspire by LEADING by example.

To be a great leader, you have to *be* the example of someone who embodies what the company's core values are and puts in the work to *be* inspiring to others to show up as their best selves every day. After all, a good leader is always lifting people up and encouraging them to live up to their fullest potential.

A great leader is forever growing and changing and challenging themselves to do better. Think of it like an iPhone software update: even new processes and goals rolled out need to have the "bugs" worked out through updates. There is always room for improvement. It's the leaders who aren't up for the challenge to make the changes needed that you should be truly concerned about because being a great leader today takes self-reflection and tenacity to be better than you were yesterday. You have to willingly and regularly challenge your own narrative.

Inspire Your Employees

After all, if the expectation is that employees show up consistently as their best selves in order to meet, and exceed, metrics/KPIs (key performance indicators) and perform profit-driven activities, the same should be asked of company's leaders.

Employees are not interested in hearing "how it has been done in the past." They're looking for transparency, awareness, and impact. They're expecting evolution in the workplace and, if employers want talent at the top of their game, then they need to understand the expectation is the same from an employee to their employer nowadays.

Companies are so focused on their brands being well received in the market by consumers, by customers, and stakeholders, that sometimes the focus on being the best internal brand gets lost in the shuffle, and that's a big problem today for employees.

Part of being a strong leader is also acknowledging your own weaknesses and then surrounding yourself with trusted advisors who round out your knowledge gaps while not losing sight of doing things the right way by using best practices.

That means leaders need to put in the work to show up as the best version of themselves on a daily basis. Because if they don't, someone else will, possibly a competitor, and then the expectation for top talent on staff will be an unrealistic one. The truth is people are drawn to great leaders so, once your leaders start to put in the work to be their best selves, the top talent will find you. In fact, they'll likely be falling over themselves to come and work for the company they've heard such great things about from their friends, family, and/or community. Finding top talent comes easily when employees feel inspired by and learn from excellence.

If the pandemic taught us anything, it's that people want to like going to work. They want to like what they're doing and who they're doing it for. Your internal brand is important as a positive workplace culture and applicant experience always draws top talent in. However, it's the leaders that inspire top talent to stay long-term and perform at their highest level. Which means your leaders need to consistently be putting in the work not only to make their team and workplace better but also to make themselves better.

But, how do you attract the best talent when you're not outwardly known as the best in the industry? You put in the work.

No one said it would be easy, but it certainly is rewarding. Being the best version of yourself means you stay true to yourself even if no one is watching, and showing up as your best self, even when it's hard to.

We, at Strategic Talent Resources, would love the opportunity to help you attract and retain top talent. We would be happy to work with you and your team to determine which areas your business needs support when it comes to your applicant and employee experiences. Please take the opportunity to reach out to us today to schedule a discovery conversation at: hello@strategictalentresources.com

Joy Poli
About the Author

Joy Poli of Strategic Talent Resources is a highly acclaimed Human Resources professional with over 20 years of expertise in talent acquisition. As the founder of Strategic Talent Resources, she has established herself as a trusted partner for businesses seeking effective recruitment and retention strategies. Joy and her team build the infrastructure necessary to attract and retain top talent.

With her exceptional ability to connect people and her dedicated work ethic, Joy has earned a stellar reputation for matching individuals with the right opportunities and fostering valuable business relationships. She excels at understanding the specific needs of clients and candidates, ensuring that the most suitable candidates for each organization.

www.strategictalentresources.com
www.oinnero.com

 linkedin.com/in/joypoli

Chapter 8
Four Stories
Pathways to Becoming an Opportunity Champion

"Business opportunities are like buses, there's always another one coming."

— Richard Branson

By Lynn E. Miller

Growing up, I was taught hard work was key to achieving any goal. My mantra was "Do whatever it takes." When hard work didn't get me the results I wanted, my efforts stalled. Overwhelmed and upset, I often sought my father's advice about what to do next. In those moments, my father asked me this question: "Why stop when you're halfway across the pool—the distance is the same whether you continue or turn around and go back?"

From that moment on, whenever I got "stuck," my father's question reminded me what to do. Over time, I built the persistence, and tenacity to "see things through" throughout my career. Over time, all that hard work led to burnout. At my lowest point, I questioned my ability to pursue *any* profession.

In 2018, I decided to start substitute teaching in underserved neighborhoods. Contributing to the education of underserved children gave me purpose. I enjoyed helping these children learn and saw the difference I was making every day.

Deep down, I knew substitute teaching could not be a long-term plan. I enjoyed contributing to those who needed and valued the help. The truth was, the work was too exhausting and didn't provide enough income.

In February of 2020, I realized if I could recreate the feeling of serving a bigger purpose while earning more money, I could start a new career. Similar to others like me, I was later in my career and "not done yet."

A month later, the pandemic hit. My attention shifted back to entrepreneurs, who I always enjoyed helping. I just wasn't sure what they needed that would add value.

What I *did* know was that speakers, workshop leaders and consultants, who normally delivered their content in person, had a problem they needed to solve.

I became inspired by what "making a difference" would look like for these groups of people. It ignited feelings I hadn't experienced before—joy and passion! The thought of helping professionals who are later in their careers and "not done yet" gave me the purpose I needed to move forward.

Fast forward to June 2023. Deciding to write this chapter for the Inner Circle Leading from Within collaborative book motivated me to take my writing skills to the next level. The leadership trait I chose was "opportunity champion." I felt a connection to these words personally, and was curious about their actual definitions.

First, I looked up "opportunity" in the dictionary. It said, "A situation or condition favorable for attainment of a goal" and, "To accept or pursue an opportunity (to do something) with clarity or conviction." The part about "conviction" resonated with me.

For years, I wrote about my commitment to helping entrepreneurs grow their businesses exponentially.

Then I looked up "champion" in the dictionary. It said, "Someone who fights for, or speaks for another person in favor of a cause." There it was—my purpose!

Since the pandemic started in March of 2020, I've used my expertise, creativity and curiosity to fight for speakers, workshop leaders and consultants who wanted to grow their businesses. Once I attached the name "opportunity champion" to my work, the writing juices started to flow.

Stories and Lessons Learned About Being an Opportunity Champion

Once I started this chapter, I couldn't help but wonder about successful colleagues who had more experience and insights as opportunity champions. I invited three leaders to discuss how this presents for each of them. I asked each of them a series of questions.

- Why do you consider yourself an opportunity champion?
- What story/example can you share about how you built on past success to serve a bigger purpose?
- How are you moving forward to make a difference in the world?
- What advice do you have for others?

I hope you find these questions and stories helpful as you consider next steps in your business.

Meg Bear, Former President of a Global Software/Services Company

(on sabbatical)

In 2019, Meg stepped into the job as President of a large global software/services company. Meg led the company's mission to provide an environment where work:

- Is valuable and creates mobility.
- Provides opportunities to learn from each other and make sure technology respects humanity vs. diminishing opportunity.
- Pays attention to which voices are missing and gives them a voice vs. keeping the opportunity from them.

Opportunity Champion

During our conversation, Meg shared her belief that everyone has the potential to be an opportunity champion. Her unique experience as the first in her family to attend college and secure a professional role drives this belief. Meg seized this opportunity after decades of experience with startups, established software/services companies, and purpose-driven software solutions.

Building on Past success to Serve a Bigger Purpose

When she stepped into her new role as President, Meg had a unique opportunity to build on the company's success, and used it as a platform to accomplish more. She saw this role as an opportunity to change a category, which until then was quite dated, to something more meaningful that would require technology changes.

Prior to making the technology changes in the company's software, Meg went on a quest to work with global leaders and clarify what it takes for individuals to do their best work and show up as their best selves.

Making a Difference in the World

Through her work, Meg intentionally created sustainability for what was known as a rather unpopular profession AND the future of work. Global customers contributed to this initiative which resulted in a new connection between the department and the workforce on innovative ways to support and equip people so that they can contribute to the business.

The *new* future of work included:

- Creating a workplace where opportunities don't feel diminished by anyone.
- Including voices that are currently missing in Diversity, Equity and Inclusion.
- Calling out who opportunity is being given to vs. being withheld from.
- Identifying where the globe can help us in our ability to support each other with humanity/compassion/curiosity/humility.

Meg and her team also saw this initiative as an opportunity to address the growing skills gaps and build a solid foundation for what the future of work could look like.

Meg offers this advice: "It is my deep belief that our most important goals should be to find what we are uniquely good at and figure out how to use that in the service of others."

This story illustrates how Meg became an opportunity champion by building on a global company's past success, and her own.

Sean Stowers, CEO, WeLearn

While working in a large company for 18 years, Sean kept asking himself, "What is the opportunity I want?" It wasn't long before Sean came to the scary realization that he wanted to start and build his own company, WeLearn Learning Services and Workforce Development. When he started WeLearn, Sean included a written commitment to be mission/goal/brand aligned. This resulted in solutions that demonstrated empathy by making the learning experience more humane and compassionate.

Why do you consider yourself an opportunity champion?

"Personally, being an opportunity champion means **not** taking "no" for an answer. In terms of my practice and the work we do here, being a champion for accessibility is really important.

"For me, accessibility is as much about the technical aspects of accessibility in terms of the learner being able to use screen readers or having subtitles, as it is about really respecting the learner and knowing the learner.

"Our commitment is to make sure everybody has equitable access to learning. Some people grow up not believing they can be successful learners because there are no support structures or people in their lives that say, 'You can do this.' I come from a place of compassion that not everyone has the same relationship with learning as me."

What story/example can you share about how you built on past success to serve a bigger purpose?

"After 20 years working for large global learning services companies, I knew I wanted to get up every day and work with people I love to do really cool stuff, which led me to that entrepreneurial moment.

"I believe it's really important in learning, particularly learning we build for our clients, that even if every learner isn't able to master what we teach, they have an equal opportunity to engage in the learning experience. That could be reading level, seeing representation of themselves in the material, or being able to complete assessments engineered in a way that is not overly complex.

"We recognize everyone comes into learning from different places and invite them into the experience of learning in a more welcoming way."

How are you moving forward to make a difference in the world?

"Being open minded and curious for me means representing more voices from an ability, gender, race and educational point of view and has a measurable impact on client success. One example of this is using the *Hemingway App* to adjust the content the team writes for readability. I also remain intensely curious and passionate about being an opportunity champion for getting in front of progress by embracing new technologies."

What advice do you have for others?

"Some days it takes a lot to quiet the inner voice that says, 'You're going to fail today' and instead say, 'This is my opportunity. Everything is going to continue to be good.' You have to be your own cheerleader, maybe your own therapist, and your own gatekeeper. This is all in service of protecting your time to champion the opportunities you want to advance."

This story illustrates how Sean used the mastery of existing talents and took his talents in a new direction.

Loretta Stagnitto, Loretta Stagnitto Leadership Associates

Opportunity Champion

After working as a leadership coach for over 25 years, Loretta knew she wanted to find ways to serve an additional group of directors who report to the senior executives she coaches.

Loretta received feedback from clients that her coaching added value. That's when she knew she wanted to use technology to reach an additional audience and be more competitive.

Building on Past success to Serve a Bigger Purpose

While working as a marketing leader in the technology industry, Loretta learned about the practice of expanding on revenue opportunities by creating new products—also known as "brand extensions." As her coaching business grew, Loretta wanted to incorporate this practice into her business.

Making a Difference in the World

Loretta wanted to deliver similar value to more people. That's when she decided to turn her services into products so that she could help accelerate leadership development at the director level and beyond.

Loretta offers this advice: "Step back and think of yourself as a consumer. When you put yourself in the consumer's shoes, it will give you clarity that you can't do it alone. When you work with experts, be open to their process."

This story illustrates how Loretta used expansion to fulfill her opportunity champion goals.

My Own Story

While reflecting on my experiences, a few natural abilities quickly came to mind. I was a continuous learner, naturally curious, thrived on creativity, and embraced the unexpected. To me, seizing opportunities felt like a "no brainer," or so I thought.

Early in my career, I don't recall having a greater purpose when going after what I wanted. I did, however, have dreams of being great using some of my natural talents. Younger me assumed hard work and practice would be enough to eventually be great.

I focused on talents most people I grew up with didn't want to pursue. Older me eventually learned that dreams about being great also required writing down goals, discipline, sacrifice, being coachable, tenacity, failing, and having the guts to fail again.

Here's what happened. My first dream was wanting to be an opera singer. Ten years of training, coaching, along with 10,000 hours of practice and performing taught me my first important lesson.

Lesson Learned #1: *Having natural talent and learning how to use it doesn't mean it will bring you joy.*

My dream to be a successful opera singer ended.

Next, I dreamed about being successful in business. I pursued a career in retail management and corporate training in a billion dollar company. I was surprised at how successful I was at growing a business and developing managers. Three years later, the company promoted me to corporate training.

When the time came to have children, retail management no longer interested me.

Lesson Learned #2: *Being successful at something doesn't translate to bringing you joy.*

For the next 15 years, while raising two children with my husband, I *finally* discovered a bigger purpose. My role in enterprise sales for the learning technology industry was a career worth pursuing because I could help financially support my family.

Long hours, weekends, and travel were part of the table stakes to achieving this goal. I won awards that led to fun trips to beautiful destinations. Did it bring me joy? Definitely not. Something was missing with the choices I made.

I needed to try something new and experimented with different ways to capitalize on a few other strengths like writing and conference development.

Lesson Learned #3: *Experimenting without a bigger purpose or wanting to make a difference for others leads to dead ends.*

Experiencing a Mindset Shift

In 2020, we all faced the unexpected--the pandemic. Many reacted to this experience with fear and resentment.

I embraced it and, at the same time, experienced a mindset shift. The moment I realized the pandemic was here to stay, I knew 20+ years of experience in learning technology and business development could be a winning combination. It felt like a light shining through the crack of a slightly opened door.

Quickly, visions of groups of people I wanted to serve emerged. Seasoned professionals struggling to find new ways to continue working and expand what business they already had as speakers, facilitators and consultants.

I imagined collaborating with these experts on strategies for growth so that their expertise would be more accessible, available and affordable to more companies.

This was the bigger purpose I was missing! Each day, I got more excited about fulfilling this vision. Within two years, one offer turned into three different services.

That's when I created a framework that helped seasoned professionals decide on their right signature online program, easy.

Lesson Learned #4: *Embracing the unexpected helped me discover my bigger purpose!*

I'm solving the problem of re-purposing and transforming content that takes years, maybe a lifetime, to develop into accessible, available and affordable learning experiences for an expanded audience. This allows me to make a difference in a couple of ways:

- I can help more people identify pathways to grow your businesses exponentially.
- Our work to make your content more accessible, available and affordable could positively impact more groups of people in the world.

Conclusion

I hope sharing my story and stories from my colleagues helped you realize that curiosity, creativity, finding what we were uniquely good at, and embracing the unexpected were paths to becoming opportunity champions.

Once we acknowledged our natural talents, we identified one or more pathways to move forward as opportunity champions.

These pathways included:

1. Discovering why we wanted to be an opportunity champion for others
2. Building on past successes and expanding on what we already know how to do to serve a bigger purpose.

3. Mapping out a path forward to make a difference in the world.

Now it's your turn to use your natural talents.
Why? Because you're already your own Opportunity Champion! Below are three next steps you can take:

- Imagine what it would be like when your business brings you joy and embrace the unexpected–it will open up a world of opportunity!
- Follow the advice from my fellow opportunity champions.
- Choose one of the three pathways my colleagues and I used.

Next, identify how your unique combination of know-how and mastery can help you be an opportunity champion for others.

How did this chapter help you discover the opportunity champion you are already? Email me what you discovered at lynn@straighttalkwriter.com,

Subject Line: Opportunity Champion. I can't wait!

Lynn E. Miller
About the Author

Lynn E. Miller is the founder of **Straight Talk Writer LLC** and author of the *10x Your Expertise strategic consulting process*, with the mission to help seasoned professionals who want to transform keynotes, presentations, workshops and consulting materials into online programs that are available, accessible, and affordable and transformative to an expanded audience.

Lynn is a learning technology and business development expert with the innate ability to listen for the bigger purpose behind people's expertise, capture how they want to be known, and turn that intelligence into compelling online learning experiences that lead to a mindset shift and behavior change.

In her free time, Lynn plays tennis, spends time with friends and family and travels with her husband to visit their family.

linktr.ee/lynnmiller6

Chapter 9
Success Traits in Action
Building a Fierce Network

By Kim Kleeman

"I don't want to go to an alien movie." At 16 years old, I slumped down in the car as my parents picked me up from work. They had set up a ruse, telling me after my 8-hour work day, that I was about to sit in a movie (for my little brother) about aliens. I was livid and tired, and not interested. As we drove home, I thought about all the other things I wanted to do other than go to a kid's movie, when my dad said we had to stop at home quickly to grab a sweater for my mom who would be cold in the movie. As we pulled into the driveway and I wiped away the tears and looked up, I noticed something odd. Was that my two best friends Katie and Kim on the roof of my house? I was... confused. What was going on?? As I walked from the car to the house, I looked inside the big bay picture window to see a sea of friends. A surprise party? For me??? I was... well, emotional. I walked into that group of friends, planned by my besties, many of whom didn't know each other. There was a church youth group, and my varsity gymnastics friends, my theater friends, my grammar school friends, some of my cousins, and so many more. My favorite people all in one place. The best memories of that night were that

1. I couldn't stop crying, and
2. Different groups of people came together to celebrate with me.

It was a feeling I still wrap around myself when times are tough. I am loved. I am cared about. I hope to show the same to others in this journey we are all taking. It's special to be part of a caring community and I hope those who are looking to build one or be in an impactful one find their way.

Building Strong Networks

During my career over the past years, I've had the pleasure of being part of great teams, and really strong networks and I have developed friendships with work colleagues that have lasted the test of time, even if things didn't always go well in the end. There are people I hang out with regularly that I had to let go as an employee due to turbulent times, and there are advisors who I have paid to be in my life whether it's insurance or legal, or even real estate. In business, and in life, we all experience ups and downs. We know someone who had to make tough decisions in stressful times. It may even be something they experience more than once as a business owner or leader- another layoff, another tightening of the budget. Or even worse, like the end of businesses in tough times, the end of a client/vendor relationship, the end of an employer/employee relationship, the end of a partnership, or more. It's not all perfect but I can point to important people in my network who have worked through the stuff that makes the entrepreneurial or leadership journey a tough, lonely one sometimes. I cherish these relationships and work hard to keep them up. I have one-on-ones on my calendar, I create opportunities to go out and have fun when I can, and I make sure my power partners know I appreciate them.

These are the traits of success that I've identified and have put into the curriculum at *Accelerate Successfully,* a business ecosystem built for its clients, and much of this is shared with the *Inner Circle*. My sister, Joy Poli, and I wanted to create a place for our favorite referral partners, and our clients to grow together and to build each other up. We wanted a place where we could feature and market one another's events, as well as come together and connect, send each other business, and build out new offerings or go after a client together to make the outcome more efficient and better for their company's goals. My sister, Joy Poli, and I started this community 5 years ago. It's been quite the ride from over 38 in-person events in one year as well as going completely virtual during the pandemic, and now finding our stride both nationally and internationally.

Throughout these chapters, authors wove these traits of success into their stories and wisdom. They interpreted them to be something meaningful in their life, showcasing that they've mastered them over time. Most times with some life lessons along the way.

Through *Accelerate Successfully, we* created the framework and philosophy of the *Inner Circle* brand and membership. It is a community built to aid those who want to grow and need resources in their own network. In my eyes, each member is truly a client of Accelerate Successfully since the curriculum, the masterminding, and the facilitating are all elements of the platform.

Leading in Your Own Network

When we invite new potential members to the Inner Circle, we are looking for leaders who want to be in a network with other great leaders. That means they need to grow their own communities or be willing to try. It means being a leader in your industry. It means sharing knowledge and advice with others when they are seeking it. It means showing up, following through, and making others a priority in the give-and-take world we live in.

For someone to be a leader with a great network they need to think about how often they give and how often they receive in their business dealings.

Building a network as an adult became something I thrived in and became very good at because I like making friends and learning about people and their stories. I genuinely like people. The work I put in is work I enjoy, and of course, Joy does the things I am not strong at or our team does the rest. We think it's worth the time and effort. Consider building your network so you can increase that net worth, as the saying goes.

But what is this network for and why?

First, a reminder that in your network there are people who "know" you, who see you, who check in on you, who want to catch up, who want to join in, who want to plan and travel and sing and dance and cry together. A true community. They are your first line of defense. If you need something, you call them - your mom, cousin, best friend, partner, or other people in your circle. I didn't take mine for granted and watched how others grew theirs. It was clear mine was going to be home-grown, not from a Big Ten school, a sorority, or even one school (try 2 high schools and 4 colleges).

But make no mistake, this means you have to do the same for them, giving back, and taking time to show them in actions that you care, giving sometimes more than you feel comfortable with - being a giver with no strings attached. Adopting this mindset is one of abundance and love and is a "go-high" instead of a "going low" kind of approach. It may not come naturally but ultimately this is one of the best ways to go through this life, one with deep friendships, meaningful work, and teams that make it all worthwhile. The *Awareness* of this success trait and the work you do for it is key to being in a successful networking community. *Focused empathy* gives you a place to give people grace - and many people need that now more than ever. This trait of success is one of those traits that is honed while no one is watching. Being someone to count on is key! So how do you find those awesome types of people?

For me, I kept growing those that I knew and trusted and, of course, the birth of social media helped with that expansion as well. Also, it's my observation that those who are best at networking are leaders in relationship building. People like them and want to spend time together- on the golf course, grabbing a drink, and introducing them to a client with certainty that this is the person to trust, and who can help you. They have their own network because they care about, cultivate, and grow those relationships. You know the one- the guy who always gets everyone together for the Bears game, or a reunion, or an outing. They are the glue to most groups and communities and there are far too few of us out there.

Shhh, those who ask what's the secret, are waiting to hear an easy answer but it's the same integrity-driven work, day in and day out. Such as welcoming in new contacts, trusting first, even giving first, or identifying a risk that is worth taking with a new partner, over and over again. And yes there are burns and losses but there are also life-long clients, friends, and colleagues in your industry to get to know and love. There is business and repeat clients and more business in these relationships. It's the key to a successful and long consultative career.

Many of the leaders in the Inner Circle are leaders in their own right. They have their own communities, they had many contacts before they came into the IC. I mean that's actually an important prerequisite for a portion of our membership. For the most part, there's a connector DNA to our members: they welcome it and want to meet others, they want to refer business, and they want to brainstorm on ways to collaborate. That's when you know you have something special! Starting to look around at who you are surrounding yourself with is a key element to building the best group of people around you.

We built the concept of the various circles we have in this community based on the way people best work. Some circles are focused on an industry like HR or Marketing, and some are based on target clients or outcomes like the Whale Hunters and the M&A squad. There are mastermind groups that meet monthly and create transformational relationships and increase their business outcomes because of it.

As a business coach, with *Accelerate Successfully,* I work with business leaders to become the best leaders they can be and to reach their goals, revenue or otherwise. Many of my clients have doubled their businesses, but more rewarding is that they take vacations, write books, and have time to network. They have time to go to their kid's school events, and they can determine what is needed for each season of their life. And because they have built a business in order to live the life they love, they can prioritize others and not live in constant survival mode. And when they are in that place of need, there are others to meet with, talk to, and get reassurance from. Way better than going at it all alone. It can be hard over the years. Our awards program is designed to recognize members who embody these success traits! It gives all of us something to work towards too!

Growing Leadership Skills While Networking

Nobody's perfect, and many people are afraid to refer someone to a client because they are worried about their reputation. This is understandable but truly not in the best interest of the small business community. If you know someone who can help another person, it is imperative you make that connection.

In school, students are given direct feedback regularly. Teachers give grades, write comments on papers, have office hours with students and even speak to their parents when needed. But as adults in the real world, and those that are leaders or are entrepreneurial, there's no constructive feedback, unless we ask for it. Sure we may get an angry customer from time to time, and handle that, but overall, finding ways to improve comes from people who care to tell you. In our community, we encourage those critical conversations. You know the ones we typically avoid? Yes, but they are oh-so-important. Trusting those that you refer in, especially to your own clients, means how they interact affects your reputation. Have you ever been embarrassed that you've made a connection and then the person you introduced didn't respond? Or how about not understanding how someone works and how they price their services? Many times it's not a good look to have someone you referred make your client feel bad or not work out. So how do you handle these types of things? How well do you need to know the person you referred to give them the feedback, like your pricing is too high, or that you offended them in the way you asked for payment? *Communication* is one of the most important of the success traits in business.

Our community is designed to help our members gain a greater sense of the business landscape, to find their way through in an accelerated authentic manner. We provide opportunities for members to find their power partners and refine their offerings. We give feedback on pitches and new websites. We share ideas on how to improve when asked. Oftentimes we put on free webinars for members to educate them on something that will make a marked difference in their lives, like the creative process or financial tools, or how new hiring practices will affect business owners or their employees.

We find this to be of utmost importance and welcome others who agree to check our community out!

Why IC?

Super connectors recognize one another easily and when they get together it's simply magnetic! Joy and I started the *Inner Circle* for a few reasons. First, we needed a community to bring our clients to, she working in HR with larger companies, and my business advisory clients as well as all of the resources I would regularly recommend to someone anyway.

When we invited people in 5 years ago, we knew it was going to be something special, and it has morphed into a true community, driven by the right things, what members want and need, what their clients want and need, and a way to stay connected enough that we could pick up the phone when it was time for any particular resource. I spent a ton of time connecting people 1:1 and it became clear I needed to grow those connections exponentially as my business coaching roster grew.

It's really important to make sure those connections are strategic, worthwhile, and timely. This means our Inner Circle needs to be "inner circling," or working together without Joy and I creating the space each and every time. Once we empowered others to help us grow those spaces, more and more members stepped forward to take on a piece of this and make it just the thing that other networking groups were missing, like some key elements of how human nature works such as *collaboration and not competition* as a philosophy. Maybe we have something special or maybe it's just like any other good network. Either way, it works for us. I am pleased in the 5 years we have been building this community, we feel like it is finally taking shape nicely.

The IC today is not the one we started. Joy and I let go of a lot of different iterations on how the IC works. Now we have it in pretty good shape and welcome trusted advisors, CEOs, consultants, speakers, and coaches to check us out. It's quite the group and we are very proud of the leaders within this group. They exude the traits of what we are all about. Many of them are authors in this book!

Our pillars are focused on growing better, more impactful leaders who are up-to-date on all aspects of business, who are looking to continue to grow and learn, and who want to take their leadership skills to the next level or to share what they've learned along the way.

Leaders From Within

Over time our members grow in their leadership skills, their sales and marketing skills, their speaking and writing skills, and they learn how to carve out their own path amongst their peers. Our goal is that we are *better together*. Encouraging one another, giving back together, gaining authentic and well-meaning feedback from each other and so much more. Who better than the people who care about you to give you honest feedback? They want to see you succeed. We all do.

Each member has access to so many ways to interact and grow, but it is up to them to engage and to reflect on their journey in order to fill the gaps they may have in their capabilities.

Our members are so dedicated to this that they speak regularly, take a phone call from a member to help them with a situation or issue, and of course, our members refer or help each other's clients- in a trusting and reliable way. Talk about integrity as a consultant; imagine referring one amazing person after another to a client who truly needs help. That's the Inner Circle way.

As a business coach, and one who helps others seek clarity, solve business problems, and grow their leadership to reach their dreams, having this amazing community is such a gift. My clients feel the love right away and when someone becomes a client, they are given a year-long membership so they can continue to grow even if they've ended their engagement with my coaching earlier. This community, along with my free monthly mindset workshop combined with the 1:1 coaching sessions, gives my clients a well-rounded approach to business or leadership growth. It's truly a beautiful thing!

My favorite part is when there is an AHA! moment. They attend my coaching, they receive the tools needed and they start attending the events- which create opportunities. In a quick series of steps, many people have breakthroughs and build confidence to create more goals and see that their options are much more than they might've thought. It's building the life that they love!

I could fill this chapter with pages and pages of testimonials but you can go to our website for that. Instead, understanding why we built this community and who is behind this amazing group is most important. By now you have met our authors, and leaders, in the Inner Circle. Each one is unique, and so much fun to work with, and embodies the Inner Circle core values regularly. My hope is that this book, and their marketing efforts, along with ours, will lead them to you, right in your time of need.

Building Leaders in the Inner Circle

Members who are leaning into this type of community are gaining so many positive things from it. Although it still takes time (this isn't an app that you swipe right and left, ya know), our members can cut their networking goals in half. Job seekers can step in and get to know many people who can pass their resume forward, and our non-profit leaders can learn from those who have built savvy businesses and will share some advice and best practices for their needs too!

The Leaders in this book are some of those who were willing to learn, quick to pick up and grow, and who continue to break through to positive engagements on a regular basis! I'm immensely proud that they choose to be part of our Inner Circle.

Kim Kleeman
About the Author

Kim is a seasoned entrepreneur and founder of Accelerate Successfully, a business coaching practice dedicated to leaders in startups to $150 million enterprises achieving sustainable growth and scalability. In 2018, Kim, alongside her sister Joy Poli, established Inner Circle Business Network, uniting B2B CEOs, trusted advisors, and referral partners. These accomplishments led to Kim's new role, as CEO of her family's Bakery Business, SBB Labs.

Kim's reputation as a public speaker, strategic networker, sales leader, and business maven garnered her prestigious awards including Fortune 500 and Crain's 40 under 40.

Kim's leisure time includes enjoying live concerts, theatrical productions, and travel adventures.

www.acceleratesuccessfully.com

Thank You

If you have enjoyed or found value in this book, please take a moment to leave an honest/brief review on Amazon **amzn.to/49DMxGn** or Goodreads. Your reviews help prospective readers decide if this is right for them & it is the greatest kindness you can offer the author.

Thank you in advance.

Acknowledgments

A heartfelt thanks to the authors and the members of the Inner Circle, the community that has grown and attracts amazing leaders. Our hearts are full!

Red Thread Publishing

Red Thread Publishing is an all-female publishing company on a mission to support 10,000 women to become successful published authorpreneurs & thought leaders.

To work with us or connect regarding any of our growing library of books email us at **info@redthreadbooks.com**.

To learn more about us visit our website **www.redthreadbooks.com**.

Follow us & join the community.

facebook.com/redthreadpublishing
instagram.com/redthreadbooks

Other Red Thread Books

To see all our published works Visit Our Library:

bit.ly/RedThreadLibrary

Our books about writing & publishing:

Book 1

The Anatomy of a Book: 21 Book Experts Share What Aspiring Authors Need to Know About Writing, Publishing & Book Marketing

Book 2

Typo: The Art of Imperfect Creation, *Permission to do it badly*

Book 3 (forthcoming)

Story Ink: *A cyclical Methodology to write 1 or 100 books*

Book 4 (forthcoming)

Write: *An Interactive Guide to Drafting Your Manuscript*

Previous Collaborative Titles in the Brave New Voices Series:

Feisty: *Dangerously Amazing Women Using Their Voices & Making An Impact*

Spark: *Women in the Business of Changing the World - 1 sentence description*

Sanctuary: *Cultivating Safe Space in Sisterhood; Rediscovering the Power that Unites Us*

Planting the Seed: *Lessons for a Brighter Future*

Sisterhood Redefines Us (Collaborative)

We are stronger together, but we must find or create our own safety first. (10 authors)

Dangerously Amazing Women (Collaborative)

If you're ready to rewrite all the rules & start thriving, just as you are, then Feisty is a must-read! (19 authors)

Women In the Business of Changing the World (Collaborative)

Celebrating the extraordinary impact of ordinary women, women when we show up & shine in our full, unapologetic authority. (10 authors)

Write & Publish with Us as a Collaborative Author

Be the next **Red Thread Collaborative Author**: bit.ly/46Yd6Ed

We believe every story matters, not just the stories of the folx who can afford to publish them. Therefore we have built-in to our business structure scholarship funds using profits to support organizations for good in the world as well as our first-time authors anthology publishing